PROGRAMME ON EDUCATIONAL BUILDING

SCHOOLS
for
TODAY
and
TOMORROW

An international compendium of exemplary educational facilities

ORGANISATION FOR CO-OPERATION AND ECONOMIC DEVELOPMENT

Organisation for Economic Co-operation and Development

Pursuant to Article 1 of the Convention signed in Paris on 14th December 1960, and which came into force on 30th September 1961, the Organisation for Economic Co-operation and Development (OECD) shall promote policies designed:

- to achieve the highest sustainable economic growth and employment and a rising standard of living in Member countries, while maintaining financial stability, and thus to contribute to the development of the world economy;

- to contribute to sound economic expansion in Member as well as non-member countries in the process of economic development; and

- to contribute to the expansion of world trade on a multilateral, non-discriminatory basis in accordance with international obligations.

The original Member countries of the OECD are Austria, Belgium, Canada, Denmark, France, Germany, Greece, Iceland, Ireland, Italy, Luxembourg, the Netherlands, Norway, Portugal, Spain, Sweden, Switzerland, Turkey, the United Kingdom and the United States. The following countries became Members subsequently through accession at the dates indicated hereafter: Japan (28th April 1964), Finland (28th January 1969), Australia (7th June 1971), New Zealand (29th May 1973), Mexico (19th May 1994), the Czech Republic (21st December 1995) and Hungary (7th May 1996). The Commission of the European Communities takes part in the work of the OECD (Article 13 of the OECD Convention).

Publié en français sous le titre:

ECOLES D'AUJOURD'HUI ET DE DEMAIN

Preface

acknowledgements

This book provides a showcase for some of the best-designed schools in the world today. They have been selected on behalf of the OECD Programme on Educational Building (PEB) by an international jury. The schools exemplify some of the ideas that have arisen from the activities of PEB during the last five years.

The members of the jury were:

Eric Bieler, Canton of Geneva, Switzerland, Vice-Chairman of the PEB Steering Committee

Per Gunvall, Swedish Institute for the Handicapped, Harnosand, Sweden

Michael Hacker, Consultant and former Chairman of the PEB Steering Committee, United Kingdom

Jean-Marie Moonen, Fonds communautaire de garantie des bâtiments scolaires, Brussels, Belgium

Richard Yelland, Head of the PEB Secretariat, Paris, France.

The PEB Steering Committee gratefully acknowledges the help it has received in preparing this publication from the schools and education authorities concerned, and the architects who designed them. The Committee also wishes to express its thanks to those who sent in nominations for inclusion but which were not chosen for publication.

Also available

	France	Other countries*		
Redefining the Place to Learn (95 95 03 1) ISBN 92-64-14563-X, 1995, 172 pp	FF 140	FF 180	US$ 37	DM 50
Schools for Cities (95 95 01 1) ISBN 92-64-14324-6, 1995, 156 pp	FF 100	FF 130	US$ 25	DM 39
New Technology and its Impact on Educational Buildings (02 92 15 1) ISBN 92-64-13756-4, 1992, 44 pp	FF 40	FF 50	US$ 11	DM 16
Decentralisation and Educational Building Management: ***The Impact of Recent Reforms*** (95 92 01 1) ISBN 92-64-13660-6, 1992, 84 pp	FF 100	FF 140	US$ 28	DM 45

"PEB Papers" series

	France	Other countries*		
Making Better Use of School Buildings (95 96 04 1) ISBN 92-64-14880-9, 1996, 37 pp	FF 45	FF 60	US$ 12	DM 17
Secondary Education in France, A Decade of Change (95 95 02 1) ISBN 92-64-14548-6, 1995, 64 pp	FF 70	FF 90	US$ 18	DM 26
The Educational Infrastructure in Rural Areas (95 94 02 1) ISBN 92-64-14189-8, 1994, 36 pp	FF 40	FF 50	US$ 9	DM 16
Educational Facilities for Special Needs (95 94 01 1) ISBN 92-64-14098-0, 1994, 30 pp	FF 40	FF 50	US$ 9	DM 16

Periodical

	France	Other countries*		
PEB Exchange (88 00 00 1) ISBN 1018-9237, 1997 Subscription		FF 160	US$ 34	DM 48

*Export prices include dispatch via economic airmail
THE OECD CATALOGUE OF PUBLICATIONS and supplements will be sent free on request addressed either to
the OECD Publications Service or to the OECD distributor in your country

Contents

J-M Moonen

Improving the quality of educational buildings is one of the objectives of PEB (the OECD Programme on Educational Building). One way of doing this is to bring to the attention of a wide audience the ideas and recommendations that have emerged from the Programme's work on how to produce quality educational buildings at a reasonable cost. The PEB Steering Committee therefore proposed the publication of a compendium of school buildings which exemplify excellence in one or more of PEB's areas of discussion and research.

Whether architect, teacher, government agent, civil servant at national (federal), regional or local level, we all may need to inform ourselves whether changes we are contemplating in the school buildings for which we are to some degree responsible are specific or form part of a broader, indeed universal, trend.

We might simply seek reassurance that nothing inherited from the past needs to be changed. Or perhaps we may want to take a look at what is happening elsewhere and see how others design schools. What we cannot dispute is the scale of change in education or, more simply, in the different methods of learning.

If we believe in the importance of good architectural design of schools, we might be aiming, through a new organisation of space, to improve education and keep it more closely in touch with the rapidly changing society of which it is a part.

The Programme's intention therefore was to gather together descriptions of buildings which would serve as illustrations in one way or another of good architectural design and management in schools. All the OECD Member countries were invited to participate. Cases were selected by an international jury of experts who between them had many decades of experience of educational policy, school design and the management of education systems.

The fact that a school has been included does not mean that it is considered to be exemplary in all respects. Cases appear in the present ▶

publication because they seem relevant to one or more aspects of PEB's work. A building might thus be included on the basis of its innovative approach to energy management, although its external appearance might seem very ordinary.

The compendium has intentionally been restricted to examples of nursery, primary and secondary schools and buildings used for vocational education. Higher or university education and institutions providing training primarily for adults have not been included. The criteria used to select the schools included are described in the next chapter and derive from activities in the PEB Programmes of Work from 1992 to 1996.

The compendium includes both new and refurbished buildings in their entirety or in part. They range in size; some enrol fewer than 100 pupils, others serve several thousand. They cater for pupils and students of very different ages. Some are situated in rural areas, others in city centres. They have been arranged so that those catering for the younger age groups come first: thus nursery schools precede primary schools, followed by secondary schools and vocational institutions.

Despite the fact that many problems are common to all countries, the development of educational architecture has followed very different courses in different places, reflecting not only tradition and climate, but also the level of economic development. The buildings which have been included in this book are very different in their styles and in their degree of technical and architectural sophistication. They are all, in some way or other, exceptional.

Naturally there are many high-quality buildings that have been completed in recent years which do not appear in this compendium. A collection such as this cannot pretend to be exhaustive. Some countries are not represented – not because they have nothing to show – but because the call for nominations was not answered. We hope that a subsequent publication will make good this shortcoming.

Successive economic crises have eroded investment budgets to a remarkable extent. Schools of whatever level are increasingly asked to fulfil satellite educational functions: sport, cultural activities, specific programmes for local or regional industrial apprenticeships. They are seen as poles of local development. This means that their premises must be more freely available and they must constantly increase their adaptability. Many of the schools featured reflect this concern.

At the same time, funding for maintenance has been more and more difficult to come by. It is notable that in the examples which follow, the categories which relate to the good management of resources are the least well represented.

The last twenty years have also been marked by a constant and growing need to integrate each building with its site. Nowadays, this might seem obvious, but we should guard against what might, on the grounds of cost, be a recurring temptation – namely to construct industrialised school buildings of a standard type regardless of where they are situated. A concern with harmony and with integration is apparent in the design of many of these schools.

When it comes to the relationship between learning technology and the built environment we have to ask whether and to what extent new learning technologies have rendered current construction technology obsolete. Several of the examples in this book show that buildings are adapting to new technologies.

Learning to appreciate beauty is also part of the educational context. And the quality of the environment can have an effect on children, the young and not so young, as they develop in spaces built with harmony and human needs in mind. The beauty of spaces and forms and the attraction of the colours chosen, effective acoustics, carefully selected materials, well-designed lighting and green surroundings all make a contribution which few would dispute.

One could continue at great length on the subject of buildings and their relationship to educational outcomes, but you the reader are no doubt eager to judge the cases presented for yourself. We have given contact names and addresses for each building so that, if need be, you can investigate further. We hope you enjoy reading the compendium and we thank everyone who helped in its production.

J-M Moonen, on behalf of the jury

Education, in OECD Member countries as elsewhere, continues to face the challenges of rapid and far-reaching change. At the same time pressures to reduce expenditure are unrelenting. The physical infrastructure of education – the places and spaces in which people learn and teach – has an important part to play both in contributing and responding to change. Better management and use of resources is necessary if the aim of high-quality education for all is to be achieved.

The various activities of the Programme on Educational Building are all intended to achieve one or more of the following three aims:

- improving the quality and suitability of educational buildings and thus contributing to the quality of education;

- ensuring that the best possible use is made of the very substantial sums of money which are spent on the design, construction, operation and maintenance of educational buildings;

- giving early warning of the implications for educational building of changes in education and in society as a whole.

The work undertaken by the Programme during the 1992-96 period reflected the priorities expressed by those concerned with educational building in participating Member countries; and took account of the recommendations made by the meeting of the Education Committee at ministerial level in 1990 and of the work of other committees and bodies of the Organisation.

Improving the quality of educational buildings

Quality in an educational building is difficult to define in absolute terms. Some aspects, such as conformity with building codes and health and safety requirements, can be described precisely and in ways which lead to objective assessments of quality. There are other aspects which are less easily quantifiable. The aesthetics of educational buildings, their suitability for the activities which take place in them, and those elements which engender a feeling of security and belonging are examples of attributes which are highly valued but hard to specify objectively.

The conviction is strengthening in many Member countries of the OECD that both these categories of building quality have an impact, not only on educational outcomes, but on the well-being of students and teachers. Barren, forbidding buildings with treeless grounds and in generally poor condition are becoming less acceptable to many communities because they are seen as inimical to good education. There is a growing realisation of the role that educational buildings play in shaping attitudes to the environment and the contribution they can make to urban renewal.

The first five categories under which buildings have been nominated for inclusion in the compendium are:

 facilities in which design and/or layout of the buildings is felt to make a special contribution to teaching and learning;

 facilities which show especial awareness of the architectural heritage or of their surrounding environment;

 facilities which have made a particular contribution to urban renewal or to the resolution of urban problems;

 facilities which make a particular contribution to education and community life in rural areas;

 facilities which make imaginative use of buildings and grounds (for example, for environmental education).

Management of the physical resources for education

The accumulated investment represented by the educational building stock is very significant in all Member countries. Each year OECD countries devote, on average, more than five per cent of their gross national product to education. Recent work by PEB suggests that the cost of building, running, cleaning, heating and maintaining schools approaches one-fifth of that amount in many of them.

In a context of limited funding, increasing and changing demand for education, and reform in the structure of decision making, there is continuing and sustained pressure for better value for money to be obtained from the resources devoted to educational buildings. Many countries are becoming extremely concerned about issues such as the maintenance of ageing stock, vandalism, the redeployment and adaptation of buildings, the use of premises for more than one purpose and the reduction of premises-related recurrent expenditure. In many cases however even the basic information necessary for effective management is lacking.

Work in the past five years has tackled a number of aspects of these questions, and the categories under which schools have been nominated for the compendium are:

 facilities which have been exceptionally well maintained, or which are designed in such a way as to offer low-cost maintenance in the future;

 facilities where the consumption of energy is effectively managed;

 facilities which make especially effective use of space;

 facilities where imaginative reuse has been made of an existing building.

Change and its impact on educational building

Changes in the societal context of education as well as innovation in teaching and learning methods have implications for buildings and present a challenge to designers and managers. The Programme has two roles in response to such changes:

- to collect, analyse and disseminate information about innovation in educational building;

- to identify trends in society and education and their implications for educational buildings.

Developments in new educational technology, the growth of lifelong learning, new partnerships between education and industry, concern for the environment, and renewed interest in the school as a focus for community development all have implications which need to be addressed in the immediate future.

The categories for inclusion under this heading are:

 facilities which provide for effective and innovative use of new information and communication technologies in education;

 facilities which make a reality of the lifelong approach to learning;

 facilities which respond to the changing role of education in the community;

 facilities where an effective partnership has been created with business or industry.

restored mansion

Beltrame Nursery School is housed in a mansion of some historical and architectural interest. Built between 1890 and 1930 by modifying and expanding existing farm buildings, the house lies in magnificent grounds with a breathtaking view over Bologna.

The house has been extensively restored and remodelled to accommodate both the nursery school and the crèche. After consulting childcare experts, ▶

ADDRESS	via Vittorio Putti 32 40136 Bologna Italy
TELEPHONE	+39 51 330349
FAX	
TYPE OF SCHOOL	preschool
NO. OF STUDENTS	75 with 51 places in the crèche
AGE RANGE	0 to 6 years
TYPE OF PROJECT	renovation
YEAR OF COMPLETION	1995
CLIENT	Municipality of Bologna
ARCHITECT	Stefano Magagni

Above: *rear aspect, with view of city;*
Right: *main school entrance.*

the architect has succeeded in tailoring the renovation to the needs of the school and crèche by taking into account the latest teaching methods.

The nursery school is located on the first and second floors of the mansion. Two areas have been designed for each set of pupils. The first, the classroom proper, is set aside for educational and play activities and meals. The second, the atelier or art workshop, is for specialised activities. Each atelier is different, and this allows children of different age groups and classes to mix and take part in a variety of activities.

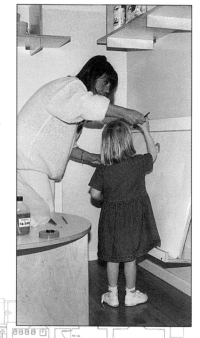

Top and bottom: *areas for play activities;*
Middle: *ground floor plan.*

The ground floor and the additional building are used for the crèche. This allows the young children easy access to the school grounds. The building also has a hall for group activities such as theatre and physical recreation.

While preserving and enriching the architectural heritage of the villa, this renovation allows the teachers to provide a highly practical teaching programme, well adapted to the new curriculum. The school is very welcoming and gives a strong impression of generosity, harmony and conviviality.

integrated town centre

Switzerland

ADDRESS
**Place du Manoir
1920 Martigny
Valais
Switzerland**

TELEPHONE
+41 26 21 24 00

FAX
+41 26 21 24 09

TYPE OF SCHOOL
**preschool, primary,
special needs**

NO. OF STUDENTS
450

AGE RANGE
0 to 12 years

TYPE OF PROJECT
new building

YEAR OF COMPLETION
1993

CLIENT
Municipality of Martigny

ARCHITECT
**Roni Roduner and
Fabrice Franzetti**

Top: *west facade;* **Above
left:** *northern prospect
facing the park.*

La Place du Manoir is in the centre of Martigny. It
was created in 1985 as part of a larger development
prooject, but no permanent buildings had been
constructed on the site. An architectural competition
was held to generate ideas for using the site more
rationally. The brief was to produce a development
that would complement the surrounding area and be
part of an integrated town centre.

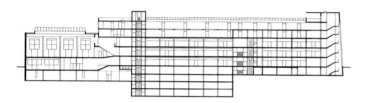

The winning design included a new park, conceived as a place of tranquillity in the heart of the town. On the park's southern side, the architects proposed a multipurpose building complex. Construction followed lengthy consultations, reflecting the need to take account of the many interests in an urban setting.

The complex includes a crèche, kindergarten and primary school, a community hall, a gymnasium, a centre for the elderly, flats and a car park. It accommodates an association for handicapped children and the municipal school board. Open 24 hours a day, there are also sports facilities for karate, wrestling, judo and boxing.

Top: *primary school classroom;* **Middle:** *east-west cross section;* **Right:** *second floor plan.*

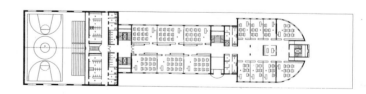

involving the family

Italy

Centro Trovamici

Advertised as "a place for children and the family", Centro Trovamici occupies the ground floor of the Leonardo da Vinci Elementary School in the historic downtown area of Empoli. Part of the building consists of the remains of a fifteenth century Benedictine convent; another building, formerly a dance studio, has been converted into a theatre for children.

The centre provides a place for education and fun for young children to come to with their parents. It also runs extracurricular activities for children and ▶

ADDRESS
Via Leonardo da Vinci, 18
50053 Empoli
Firenze
Italy

TELEPHONE
+39 571 707862

FAX
+39 571 707740

TYPE OF SCHOOL
preschool, childcare,
lifelong learning

NO. OF STUDENTS
around 350

AGE RANGE
1 year and above

TYPE OF PROJECT
renovation

YEAR OF COMPLETION
1992

CLIENT
City of Empoli

ARCHITECT
City Architect

Above: *public entrance to reception;* **Right:** *the main school building.*

◄ adolescents. Special care has been taken to make the facilities attractive both to children and to adults.

Between Tuesday and Friday, the 13 classes of the kindergarten and primary school use the computer and science laboratories, theatre, and ceramic and painting workshops. On evenings and weekends these are open for community use.

Separate, dedicated areas are provided for children under three, for those aged three to six and for those ►

Above: *the computer laboratory;* **Left:** *ground floor plan.*

aged six to eleven. A large multipurpose room is designed for use by all.

Centro Trovamici has been established as part of a wider urban renewal strategy that seeks to improve quality of life through the restoration of the city's historical buildings and gardens. The centre has made effective use of its city centre location to pursue its teaching and social objectives of developing a flexible relationship between school, family life and leisure time.

Above: *the central multi-use area;* **Right:** *children and adult helpers in the painting workshop.*

Ecole Fondamentale de Saint Vith

Belgium

ADDRESS
**Untere Büchelstrasse 10
4780 Saint Vith
Belgium**

TELEPHONE
+32 80 22 72 35

FAX

TYPE OF SCHOOL
preschool, primary

NO. OF STUDENTS
138

AGE RANGE
2 to 12 years

TYPE OF PROJECT
new building

YEAR OF COMPLETION
1995

CLIENT
**Ministerium der
Deutschsprachigen Gemeinschaft**

ARCHITECT
**Norbert Nelles and
Fabienne Courtejoie,
ARTAU scrl**

Built in an attractive rural setting, the new elementary school in St Vith is designed to take full advantage of its location. Both the internal spaces and the surrounding area are seen as learning resources, and the design emphasises the unity of the built and natural environments.

The architecture gives an impression of peace and quiet. Carefully finished stone walls and broad slate

Above: *play area for primary pupils;* **Left:** *the wing for older pupils;* **Below:** *elevation.*

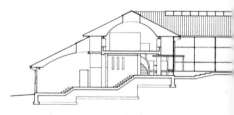

rural harmony

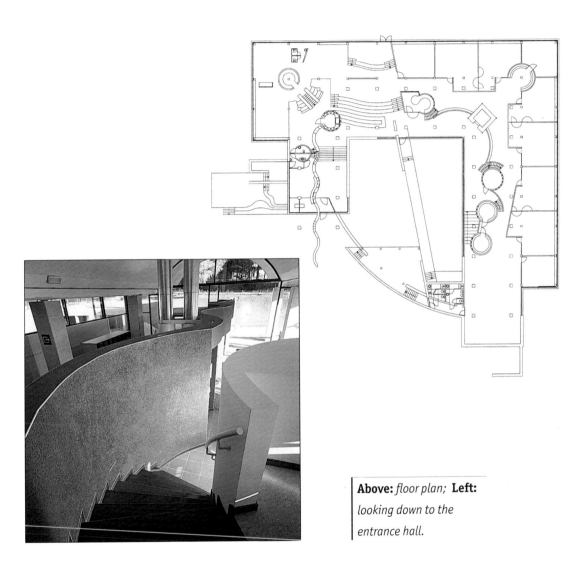

Above: *floor plan;* **Left:** *looking down to the entrance hall.*

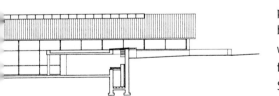

◀ roofs lend a sense of solidity and permanence. Large windows open to the courtyard and the outside world.

The nursery and the classrooms for the younger primary pupils have been housed in a wing that borders woodland. The wing for the older pupils, which also contains the gymnasium and auditorium, faces towards the secondary school and the town of St Vith, suggesting a gradual separation from the smaller child's world. ▶

◀ The reception area and the nursery recreation area
are well sheltered, so free from outside intrusion yet
accessible to parents and children. The recreation
area for the primary pupils is set amid the three wings
of the building, forming an enclosed, partially
covered, playground.

Above left: *the main
entrance;* **Above
right:** *washroom.*

Between the nursery school with its relatively
unstructured spaces and the more strictly divided
primary classrooms, a terrace opens to the outside.
Old trees have been felled to make way for more
diverse flora and fauna. In this way, children are
provided with a natural context for their earliest
years at school.

Victoria Infants School

United Kingdom

Victoria Infants School offers an unusually wide and flexible range of spaces to meet the latest developments in the primary teaching curriculum. There are areas for science, technology, computing and food technology, specially designed for young children. Teaching takes place in open class bases linked by a shared internal, top lit "street".

▶

ADDRESS
Queen's Road
Tipton
Sandwell
West Midlands DY4 8PH
United Kingdom

TELEPHONE
+44 121 557 1923

FAX

TYPE OF SCHOOL
preschool, primary

NO. OF STUDENTS
270 plus 45 nursery

AGE RANGE
4 to 11 years

TYPE OF PROJECT
new building

YEAR OF COMPLETION
1995

CLIENT
West Midlands
Urban District Council

ARCHITECT
Robin Bishop, Department for
Education and Employment, with
Sandwell Council Architects

Left: *purpose-designed furniture by the central "street".*

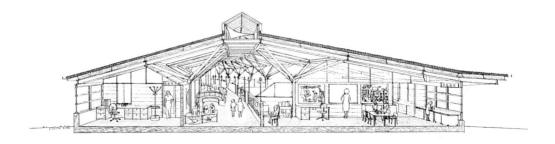

The school forms part of the renewal of an old urban, industrial neighbourhood. It makes a key contribution to community life by providing two halls, a kitchen and an innovative multi-agency centre that the council uses to serve parents and the local community. It also has nursery facilities for younger children.

Above: *cross section;*
Below: *the nursery.*

The school grounds have been designed to support outdoor teaching and environmental education. They are shared with an adjoining junior school.

The building form and construction minimises energy consumption in a variety of ways, with natural lighting and ventilation of the deep plan.

Above: *main community entrance;* **Below:** *floor plan.*

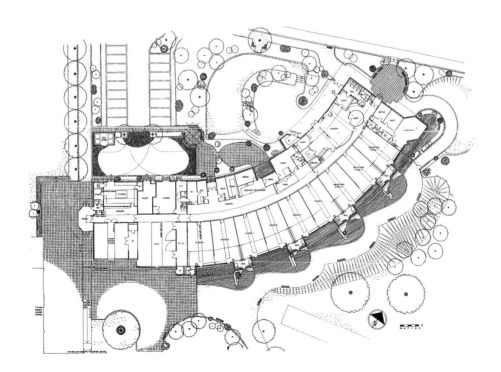

Woodlea Primary School

United Kingdom

ADDRESS

Atholl Road
Whitehill
Bordon
Hampshire GU35 9QX
United Kingdom

TELEPHONE

+44 1420 476342

FAX

TYPE OF SCHOOL

primary

NO. OF STUDENTS

245

AGE RANGE

4 to 11 years

TYPE OF PROJECT

new building

YEAR OF COMPLETION

1991

CLIENT

Hampshire County Council

ARCHITECT

Colin Stansfield Smith,
Nev Churcher and Sally Daniels,
Hampshire County Architects

Woodlea Primary School is situated in a swathe of rich woodland running down steeply from ancient Iron Age earthworks. The school is built in a natural bowl and its form, plan and substance have their origin in this landscape. The choice of materials and the natural features of the site have been exploited to produce a building that is supportive of the educational programme yet aims to be visually inventive.

▶

Above: *view of the school from the bowl;* **Left:** *contour model.*

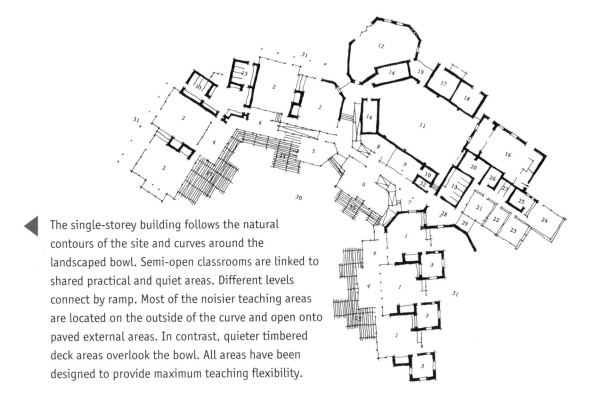

The single-storey building follows the natural contours of the site and curves around the landscaped bowl. Semi-open classrooms are linked to shared practical and quiet areas. Different levels connect by ramp. Most of the noisier teaching areas are located on the outside of the curve and open onto paved external areas. In contrast, quieter timbered deck areas overlook the bowl. All areas have been designed to provide maximum teaching flexibility.

Above: *site plan;* **Left:** *a quiet area looking into one of the classrooms.*

The link between the building and the landscape is reflected in the extensive use of timber, brick and tile. High standards of natural lighting have been achieved through the use of roof and high-level glazing. Energy consumption has been minimised by taking account of the microclimate and passive solar energy management, together with high standards of insulation.

Children at Woodlea are encouraged to take an interest in their natural environment as a learning resource. The site supports the teaching programme and environmental education. Planted with species native to the area, it includes play areas and a wildlife pond, and is linked to the adjacent woodland. The design has ensured a balance between conservation and the provision of a valuable and practical educational environment.

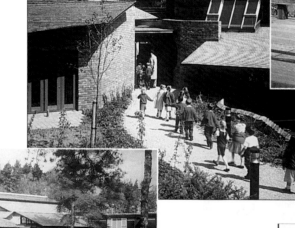

Above: *three exterior views, showing (left and right) the timbered deck areas.*

In 1993, Woodlea Primary School received the Royal Institute of British Architects' award for building of the year.

Het Kompas, Deventer

The Netherlands

Located in the old town centre of Deventer, Het Kompas replaces an older school that had become run down. Although larger than necessary for the number of pupils it served, the rooms were not suitable for modern education. To solve the problem of a shortage of development land, and to make the project financially viable, the new school has been integrated with commercial shops into a modern building.

Shops occupy the ground floor of the building. The school itself is housed compactly on the two floors ▶

ADDRESS	Broederenstraat 16 Deventer Netherlands
TELEPHONE	+31 570 611 216
FAX	
TYPE OF SCHOOL	primary
NO. OF STUDENTS	134
AGE RANGE	4 to 12 years
TYPE OF PROJECT	new building
YEAR OF COMPLETION	1992
CLIENT	Stichting het Bestuur der St Bernardusscholen, Deventer
ARCHITECT	Kristinsson

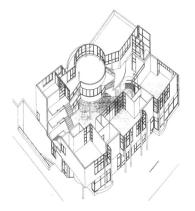

Above: *bird's-eye view;*
Left: *street view of the school above the row of shops.*

Right: *classroom facing onto the street;* **Below:** *floor plans;* **Bottom:** *the first floor play area.*

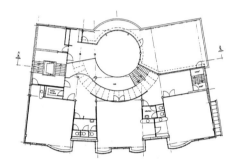

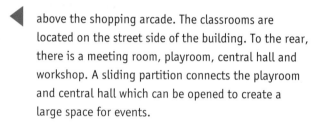

above the shopping arcade. The classrooms are located on the street side of the building. To the rear, there is a meeting room, playroom, central hall and workshop. A sliding partition connects the playroom and central hall which can be opened to create a large space for events.

There is a gymnasium, and an open play area on the roof of the shops. The play area is planted with greenery to give this inner court a luxurious character with a pleasant, child-friendly atmosphere.

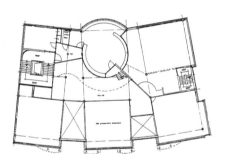

Between the classrooms there are zones for toilets and small kitchens. These are wedge-shaped, accommodating a slight bend in the street. These, together with the bow-fronted classroom windows on tall columns, produce a dynamic facade which blends well with the immediate environment.

Het Kompas, The Hague

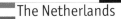
The Netherlands

ADDRESS	**Da Costastraat 40** **The Hague** **Netherlands**
TELEPHONE	**+31 70 36 55 010**
FAX	
TYPE OF SCHOOL	**primary**
NO. OF STUDENTS	**222**
AGE RANGE	**4 to 12 years**
TYPE OF PROJECT	**new building**
YEAR OF COMPLETION	**1992**
CLIENT	**City of The Hague, Education Department**
ARCHITECT	**Brasser Teeuwisse Pauw Willems**

The public primary school of Het Kompas in The Hague was the 1994 winner of the Netherlands' school building prize, an award established by the Ministry of Education and Science for the architectural design and planning involved in new construction, renovation or expansion of school buildings.

Above: *entrance from Da Costastraat;* **Below:** *first floor plan.*

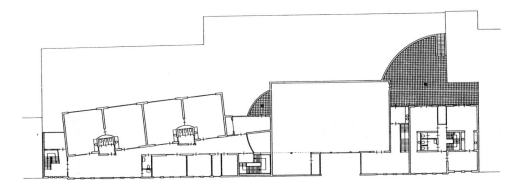

Above: *the main circulation area;* **Below:** *ground floor plan.*

With an elongated shape – the building is more than 80 metres long – the school is designed to make a positive contribution to an urban neighbourhood with many social problems. The integration of the school with the surrounding area can be seen in the fact that the auditorium, gymnasium and arts room open onto the street.

The many large windows give the school a very open impression. The main circulation area is large enough to be used for other purposes, and additional teaching spaces allow the school flexibility to respond to special needs, such as providing language learning in small groups. The building is designed to be accessible to the physically disabled and there is a daycare centre on the premises.

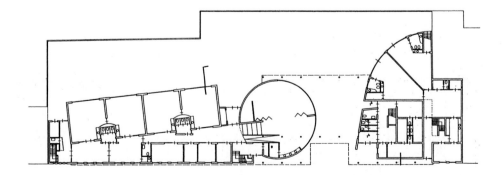

long-term adaptability

Left: *exterior view of classroom units;*
Below: *cross section of administration and resource building.*

Woodend is a new school serving a relatively young community. It was built because of the distance of other comparable schools and the growing population in the surrounding area. However, demographic projections suggest that the need for the school is only likely to be short-term. The facility has therefore been designed to allow for future use as shops and residential accommodation.

The concept of "schools in houses" has been successfully introduced elsewhere in Australia. At Woodend, however, the school has been planned and built by a private property developer. It is privately

ADDRESS
Edward Beck Drive
Sheidow Park
South Australia 5158
Australia

TELEPHONE
+61 8 322 6422

FAX
+61 8 322 7100

TYPE OF SCHOOL
primary

NO. OF STUDENTS
300

AGE RANGE
5 to 13 years

TYPE OF PROJECT
new building

YEAR OF COMPLETION
1995

CLIENT
Department for Education and Children's Services

ARCHITECT
Terence Feltus

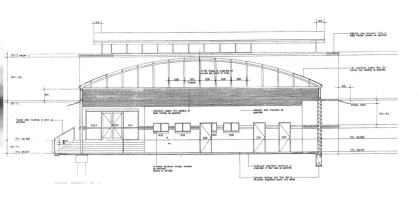

owned and leased for a fixed term to the education authorities. It is the first time the South Australian authorities have entered into such an arrangement.

The Department for Education and Children's Services had significant input in the design to ensure that the facilities would meet educational requirements in the short term. The outcome represents a negotiated balance between present and proposed uses. The architectural style has succeeded in meeting the requirements of the proposed future use yet maintaining a size and style which is not overwhelming to the users and occupants of the school.

Below left: *study area in the resource centre;*
Below right: *activity shelter in the administration and resource building;*
Bottom left: *floor plans.*

Built next to a shopping centre, the school houses a library, school offices, classrooms and teaching support facilities. The school's administration and resource building is designed to match the neighbouring shopping centre and to be compatible with local shops and offices. The classroom units, strategically placed to form a "street-scape" layout, are designed to be converted into two-bedroom homes.

The Department for Education and Children's Services has an initial lease for 15 years with two built-in rights of renewal, each of five years' duration. Thereafter, it is expected that the buildings will no longer be needed for education.

Te Kura Kaupapa Maori O Nga Mokupuna

New Zealand

A kura kaupapa Maori is a state school that provides mainstream education, but where the curriculum is delivered in the Maori language. Its purpose is to provide an acceptable alternative system of education for the Maori community, to help keep the Maori language and culture alive, and to improve educational achievement.

There are 34 state-funded kura kaupapa Maori in New Zealand. The schools are relatively small, with each

ADDRESS	132 Coromandel Street Newtown Wellington New Zealand
TELEPHONE	+64 4 389 6606
FAX	+64 4 389 6606
TYPE OF SCHOOL	primary
NO. OF STUDENTS	60
AGE RANGE	5 to 12 years
TYPE OF PROJECT	renovation
YEAR OF COMPLETION	1994
CLIENT	Ministry of Education
ARCHITECT	Paul Bennett and Kim Baldwin, AEdis Architects

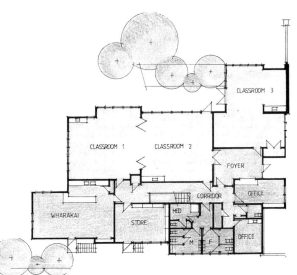

Above: *first floor plan;* **Right:** *view of classrooms from the rear.*

school enrolling about 60 pupils. This school, located in Wellington, is considered a model kura kaupapa Maori in terms of its design and functionality. It is a modern conversion of an unused school building.

Maori parents took an active role in the design of the school in consultation with the architect and the Ministry of Education. The community, for example, chose the lively colour schemes. Pupils feel that the school imbues a Maori feeling. There is a high level of satisfaction with the facilities.

Above: *teaching space;*
Left: *the "wharakai", the dining area.*

There is a fully equipped dining room and two of the teaching spaces can be opened up to provide a large meeting area. This enables the school to host community meetings and traditional formal occasions. The kura therefore provides both an important educational and cultural focus for the Maori community.

Iceland

Hvaleyrarskóli

Hvaleyrarskóli is in a newly developed and outlying part of the town of Hafnarfjördur. The single-storey school is constructed from coloured prefabricated units. It opened in 1990 and has been subsequently developed in stages as student numbers have increased.

The exposed location has influenced the design of the school, resulting in long wings that provide shelter for play areas. The form of the school separates the classrooms and recreational area of older children from those of the younger pupils. Each has its own separate entrance and playground area.

The school has three wings and is Y-shaped. The younger pupils (up to 12 years old) are housed in the first wing, the second wing has classrooms for specialised instruction and the third wing houses ▶

Above: *play areas are sheltered by the wings of the school.*

ADDRESS	
	Akurholt 1
	IS-220 Hafnarfjördur
	Iceland

TELEPHONE	
	+354 565 0200

FAX	
	+354 565 2725

TYPE OF SCHOOL	
	primary, lower secondary

NO. OF STUDENTS	
	512

AGE RANGE	
	5 to 16 years

TYPE OF PROJECT	
	new building

YEAR OF COMPLETION	
	1995

CLIENT	
	Hafnarfjördur Town

ARCHITECT	
	Ormar Th. Gudmundsson,
	Örnólfur Hall

Below: *the floor plan;*
Bottom: *multipurpose*
room; **Right:** *a corridor.*

lower secondary age groups (pupils aged 13 to 16). These three arms are connected by a central area comprising a multipurpose room, a hall, a lunchroom and lounge for the lower secondary pupils and the main entrance.

Classrooms are bright and the hallways have high ceilings. The prefabricated units are made of gypsum panels, providing good noise insulation and allowing flexibility in construction.

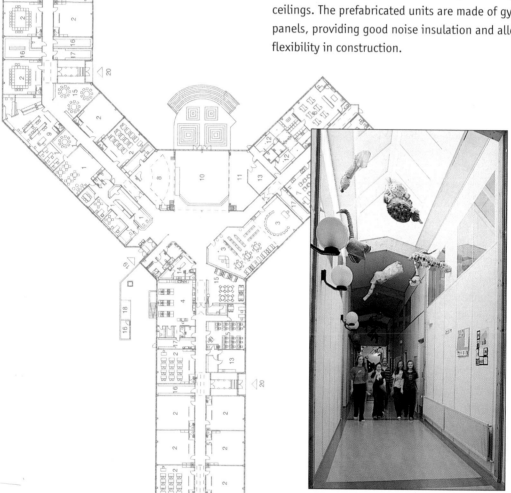

The central spaces have movable partitions so that they can be used for a variety of school and community activities. The school aims to be a social and cultural centre, and pupils, parents and teachers co-operate on at least two projects annually. Upon their completion, recitals and readings are given at gatherings attended by parents, pupils and staff.

Located in a new district with a rapidly increasing population, Setbergsskóli primary and lower secondary school can accommodate an increase in pupil numbers of up to 80 each year. When the school first opened in 1989 it had 187 pupils. Now the completed school has nearly 600 pupils who attend in two shifts.

The school is well built and architecturally pleasing. Based on a linear design, it is bright and well lit with large windows and skylights. The long hallways are used to display pupils' artwork. Each classroom has a cloakroom, washbasin and toilet facilities, a feature popular with both staff and pupils.

ADDRESS
Hlidarberg 2
IS-220 Hafnarfjördur
Iceland

TELEPHONE
+354 565 1011

FAX
+354 565 4212

TYPE OF SCHOOL
primary, lower secondary

NO. OF STUDENTS
593

AGE RANGE
5 to 16 years

TYPE OF PROJECT
new building

YEAR OF COMPLETION
1993

CLIENT
Hafnarfjördur Town

ARCHITECT
Baldur O. Svavarsson,
Jón Th. Thorvaldsson

Left: *view of north facade;* **Below:** *linear sweep of school building.*

Right: *pupils' lounge;*
Below: *first floor plan;*
Bottom: *exterior detail.*

There are fourteen classrooms for general instruction in addition to special classrooms for woodwork, sewing, home economics, art and handiwork. The building includes two smaller rooms for remedial instruction as well as a multipurpose room and hall for physical education. There is a small recreation lounge for pupils.

Equipment is of a high standard, and the furnishing and colour scheme of the school are co-ordinated. Matching shelving, side tables, and desks complement the building to harmonious effect. The pupils seem to appreciate the facilities and interior design; there is no vandalism and the school is well respected.

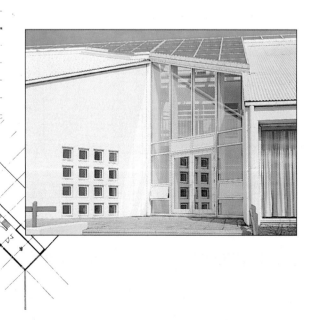

Torstorp skole

Denmark

ADDRESS	
	Torstorpvej 1
	DK-2630 Tåstrup
	Denmark

TELEPHONE
+45 42 52 85 78

FAX

TYPE OF SCHOOL
primary

NO. OF STUDENTS
9 classes

AGE RANGE
6 to 9 years

TYPE OF PROJECT
new building

YEAR OF COMPLETION
1988, 1994

CLIENT
Høje-Tåstrup Kommune

ARCHITECT
Nøhr & Sigsgaard

Architects Nøhr and Sigsgaard won an open competition in 1986 for the design of this new school. The first stage was completed in 1988. The second phase, consisting of a pre-primary school, primary school and after-school centre for children of six to nine years old, was completed in 1994. The completed school also houses a sports centre and gymnasium.

The general design concept was to provide a high level of integration between the school and surrounding residential areas. The school is the cultural centre of the community and the sports

▶ **Above:** *glass covered "street";* **Below:** *first floor plan;*

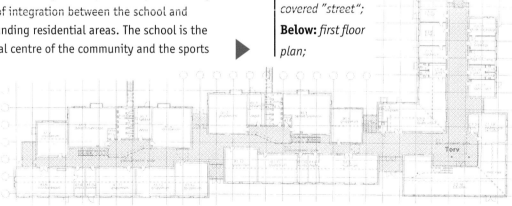

facilities, workshops, library and music room are open for use by all.

Traditional school corridors and hall have given way to glass-covered "streets" and "squares", so that classrooms become houses in a small town. The streets and squares serve the public out of school hours, providing a place for social gatherings.

Built to high-quality design and construction standards, the school uses robust materials that require little maintenance. It presents a traditional Danish image, with brick walls, concrete slab floors and tiled roofs. The glass-covered areas provide a very good source of passive solar heating and heat consumption is low in all the connected rooms.

Above: *the sports hall;*
Below: *classrooms lead out to a play area.*

Volksschule Köhlergasse

Austria

ADDRESS	
	Köhlergasse 9
	Wien 18
	Austria

TELEPHONE	
	+43 1 47 06 317

FAX	

TYPE OF SCHOOL	
	primary

NO. OF STUDENTS	
	250

AGE RANGE	
	6 to 10 years

TYPE OF PROJECT	
	new building, completed in 2 phases

YEAR OF COMPLETION	
	1987 and 1989

CLIENT	
	City of Vienna

ARCHITECT	
	Hans Hollein

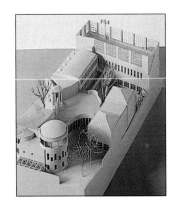

Hans Hollein has produced a rich and unique architectural solution for a city school in a built-up area. The building occupies a tiny piece of land on a steeply sloping site, yet it meets all the space requirements for a primary school of eight classes. Making good use of the available space, it offers a great variety of teaching, study and play areas.

The main entrance is on Köhlergasse. The covered entranceway, echoing a typical pattern of the area, leads to a central hall. From here, the different parts of the school are easily reached by stairways leading up and down from the hall.

▶

Left: *play areas are located on the roof;*
Above: *model of the site.*

The wing at the north of the school houses the office, medical room and staff rooms, with classrooms and leisure rooms on an upper level. Further classrooms are accommodated in the western wing, while to the south there is the dining hall with auxiliary rooms and some subject classrooms. The gymnasium is housed above garages and subject classrooms on the wing along Gentzgasse. There is a separate entrance here for community use of the gymnasium.

Top: *roof-top view;*
Middle: *classroom;*
Bottom: *north-south cross section.*

At ground level, the steepness and compactness of the site does not allow room for playgrounds or sports areas. Some open-air spaces for breaks and physical recreation are located on the roof of the building. There is also a small garden area planted with trees.

With rich and animated architecture, this building provides a remarkable infrastructure for all primary school activities. It offers a complete contrast to the "barrack-style" public sector buildings of the past.

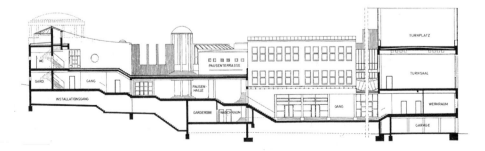

industrial conversion

Over the last 20 years, a former inner city military and shipyard area of Helsinki has been converted to residential use. Extensively renovated barracks and workshop buildings form the heart of this development and Katajanokka school has been built to serve the expanding population of the area.

The idea of placing the school in an old drill room block was first proposed in a 1972 competition aimed ▶

ADDRESS
**Laivastokuja 6
SF-00160 Helsinki
Finland**

TELEPHONE
+358 0 657 845

FAX
+358 0 3967 6390

TYPE OF SCHOOL
primary

NO. OF STUDENTS
270

AGE RANGE
6 to 12 years

TYPE OF PROJECT
adaptation and renovation

YEAR OF COMPLETION
1985

CLIENT
City of Helsinki

ARCHITECT
**Vilhelm Helander,
Juha Leiviskä Safa**

Left: *restored facade and chimney;* **Below:** *the site before renovation.*

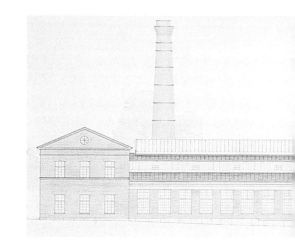

at formulating a development plan for the area. The school premises have been created partly by refurbishment and partly by new building work within existing exterior walls, dating from various periods between 1840 and 1910. The old chimney stack on the site has been restored as a monument to early Finnish industry.

A combination of old walls and spaces together with new architecture has created a well-functioning and

Top: *north-east elevation;* **Above:** *ground floor plan;* **Right:** *cross section.*

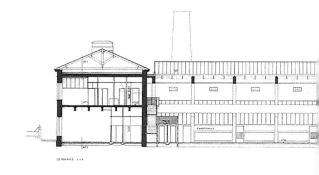

inspiring educational environment. Nine basic teaching units are housed comfortably in the buildings, whose facades have been repaired and restored. Interiors have been redecorated on the basis of the original colour schemes.

The drill hall is used as a gymnasium and assembly hall as well as for community functions in the evenings. Specialised classes such as art and music are sited in the workshop building. The heart of the ▶

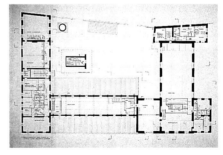

Middle: *before and after views of the former machine shop;* **Above:** *first floor plan.*

Right: *view of entrance through the yard wall;*
Below: *south-west elevation.*

◀ school is the former machine shop hall. This large space has been divided into classrooms, mostly separated by glass dividing walls and the spacious lobby area is lit by the original roof light.

In creating a new and varied school environment, the development has respected the industrial and military heritage of the site. It has given this once neglected area new life, serves the social needs of local people and is now open to all Helsinki residents.

woodland environment

Metsolan koulu

This award-winning school is discreetly sited in the grounds of an old wooded park in Helsinki. The school has been designed to meld into this woodland setting, preserving the rare and beautiful trees, and providing urban children with a harmonious and versatile learning environment.

The undulating outside wall interacts with the surrounding forest, creating a variety of outdoor spaces close to the building. The facade has the appearance of a row of small buildings linked together. Each building has a different colour, chosen to merge into the forest surroundings. The retreating effect given by the walls also reduces the visual mass of the building.

ADDRESS	Kartanomuseontie 2
	SF-00680 Helsinki
	Finland
TELEPHONE	+358 0 728 641
FAX	+358 0 728 6771
TYPE OF SCHOOL	primary
NO. OF STUDENTS	180
AGE RANGE	6 to 12 years
TYPE OF PROJECT	new construction
YEAR OF COMPLETION	1991
CLIENT	City of Helsinki
ARCHITECT	Bitumi Manner

Above: *exterior views showing the school's woodland setting.*

Built on uneven ground, the building has been terraced into three levels. The lowest level is for the gymnasium; the next level includes the changing rooms, stage and classrooms for technical work, music and handicrafts. The highest level includes the main classrooms and group activity rooms. The roof has been designed to include an opening on to a central patio.

The courtyard of the circular building is encircled by a light-filled corridor, reducing the distances between

Right: *the main corridor;*
Below: *a group activity room;* **Bottom:** *elevation showing exterior modelling.*

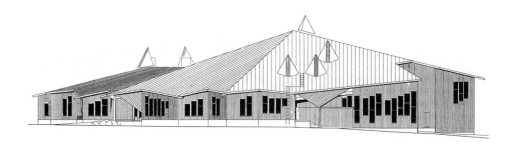

rooms. This corridor forms a series of small lobbies off the entrances and classrooms. These extend the school's usable teaching space outside the classrooms, making the corridor a suitable area for leisure and small group activity.

The angled front walls of the classrooms increase blackboard visibility nearly threefold and their hexagonal form means that different teaching situations are easier to set up.

Above: *the sports hall;* **Left:** *a lobby off the corridor;* **Below:** *cross section.*

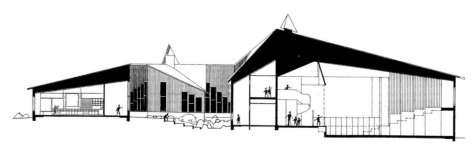

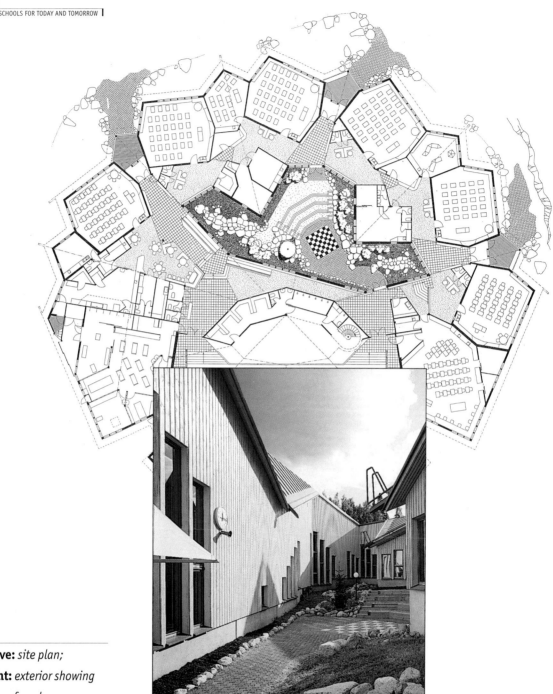

Above: *site plan;*
Right: *exterior showing the roof angles.*

In spite of its versatility, the building is fairly simple in construction and conception. All roof angles are the same both inside and out. Each building has its own colour with the same shade being used on the walls of the corridor. This makes it possible for even the youngest pupils to find their classrooms. The convertible nature of this multipurpose building supports a programme of child-centred learning.

Escola de Mértola

Portugal

Traces of Celtic, Roman, Christian, Jewish and Arab cultures can be found in and around the city of Mértola. Built in an archaeological conservation area, the new primary and secondary school lies on the site of a Roman necropolis. A sixteenth century chapel once stood in the grounds. Today, the remains of several tombs are still visible.

The new school replaces two older buildings that had fallen into disrepair. It reflects a strong desire to reflect and complement the architectural heritage and the surrounding environment, both through the design of its buildings and the way these are used in the learning process.

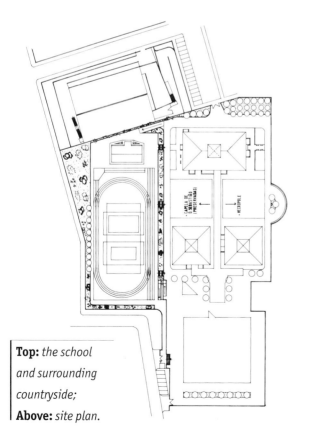

Top: the school and surrounding countryside;
Above: site plan.

ADDRESS	
	Achada de S. Sebastiao
	7750 Mértola
	Alentejo
	Portugal

TELEPHONE	
	+351 86 62803/4

FAX	
	+351 86 62805

TYPE OF SCHOOL	
	primary, secondary

NO. OF STUDENTS	
	700

AGE RANGE	
	6 to 14 years

TYPE OF PROJECT	
	new building and extension

YEAR OF COMPLETION	
	1992

CLIENT	
	Ministry of Education

ARCHITECT	
	Anabela Gomes de Carvalho,
	João Girbal and José Filipe Ramalho,
	Regional Education Office, Alentejo

The aim is to create a living museum, where students can develop an understanding of how the past has shaped both their surroundings and their culture. Pupils undertake a series of projects which bring to life the local archaeology, history and environment.

Some 500 pupils come from the surrounding villages and the school is trying to build links with these communities. There is a community centre on the school campus and there are plans to make use of a nearby church for cultural activities.

Above: *passageway running to the courtyard;* **Below:** *teaching block.*

Methilhill Primary School

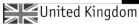 United Kingdom

This new primary school received substantial funding from the European Union for its pioneering approach to passive solar design. The building is designed to enable the effective management of energy consumption and reduce reliance on mechanical systems. Built on the site of a former farm, the 16 classroom building accommodates 464 pupils. It also functions as a social and recreational centre for the local community, both during and after school hours.

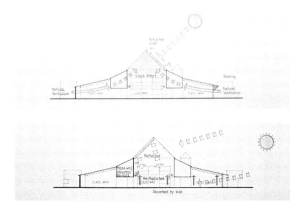

Above: *summer and winter operation of the passive solar system.*

ADDRESS	
	Sea Road
	Methilhill
	Leven
	Fife KY8 2JW
	United Kingdom

TELEPHONE	
	+44 1333 320 721

FAX	

TYPE OF SCHOOL	
	primary

NO. OF STUDENTS	
	464

AGE RANGE	
	7 to 12 years

TYPE OF PROJECT	
	new building

YEAR OF COMPLETION	
	1991

CLIENT	
	Fife Region Education Department

ARCHITECT	
	Ron Tremmel, Director of Property

The building layout is open plan with class areas grouped around two central courtyards. Unlike previous schools in the area, these courtyards are covered so that they can be used as teaching spaces for most of the year.

The building is arranged along an axis 35° east of south so that it receives the early morning sun and continues to benefit from available sunlight throughout the day. The longitudinal axis is aligned to the prevailing wind. This enables adequate ventilation to take place and minimises the winter chill factor. The windows on the facade, the clerestory glazing and the atrium roof give high levels of

Below left: *first floor plan;* **Below right and bottom:** *the central courtyards under the atrium roof.*

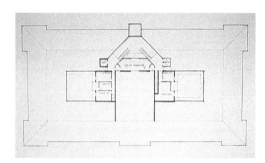

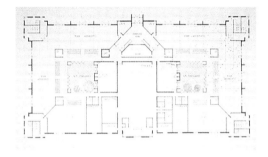

Top right: *glazing and vents in the roof;* **Above right:** *ground floor plan;* **Above left:** *teaching area.*

daylight in the occupied part of the building, reducing the need for artificial light.

The glazed areas also allow direct and reflected solar radiation to contribute to heating the class and hall areas in winter. Air in the roof space, warmed by direct solar radiation entering the atrium, acts as a source of input air for the mechanical ventilation system serving various internal rooms. Under optimum conditions this can make a significant contribution to space heating. Auxiliary heating is provided by a gas-fired boiler, radiators in the internal rooms and underfloor heating pipes in the courtyards.

Ueno Elementary School

 Japan

ADDRESS
**6-16-8, Higashiueno
Taito-ku
Tokyo
Japan**

TELEPHONE
+81 3 384 5356

FAX

TYPE OF SCHOOL
primary

NO. OF STUDENTS
316

AGE RANGE
7 to 12 years

TYPE OF PROJECT
new building

YEAR OF COMPLETION
1991

CLIENT
Taito Ward Board of Education

ARCHITECT
Shouzoh Uchii

Built in a high density suburb of Tokyo, Ueno Elementary School makes good use of its restricted site. The available land area is fully used, with the buildings extending to the fringes of the site. A large, functional and very attractive area at the centre of the project provides an impression of space.

The buildings are designed for use by the whole community. As well as the primary school, there is a daycare centre, kindergarten and community centre on the site. The school is also one of the principal centres for lifelong learning in Taito-ku.

Above: *view from the street;* **Right:** *library corner.*

Left: *multipurpose room for community education;* **Below left:** *computer room;* **Below right:** *floor plans: basement (top), second floor (lower).*

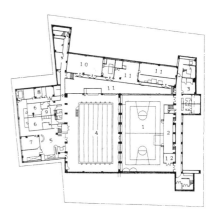

The layout allows the school to adopt a variety of teaching methods. In the main school building, there are classrooms for six grades. Each classroom is adjacent to an open space designated for group and individual learning and equipped with personal computers. The main building also houses the library and a learning resource centre. The school is able to receive satellite broadcasts and there is a separate computer room for community use.

By offering a wide range of social, sporting and cultural facilities, the school plays an important role in the local urban community. Its facilities include an indoor swimming pool, gymnasium, library, concert hall and medical centre.

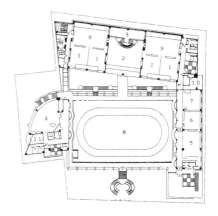

Askrova skule

Norway

| ADDRESS
6923 Tansoy
Flora kommune
Norway

| TELEPHONE
+47 57 745 130

| FAX

| TYPE OF SCHOOL
preschool, primary

| NO. OF STUDENTS
20 (plus 10 in the kindergarten)

| AGE RANGE
7 to 13 years

| TYPE OF PROJECT
new building

| YEAR OF COMPLETION
1991

| CLIENT
Flora kommune

| ARCHITECT
Kjell Hareide

Right: *the front of the school, facing the sea.*

Askrova is a small island off the west coast of Norway. Located in the isolated fjord district, the island is a thirty minute sea journey from the small town of Florø. There are 150 residents.

Built on the remains of an old school building destroyed by fire in 1989, the new school has been designed to integrate a primary school with a kindergarten. In order to maintain continuity, the stone walls from the cellar of the old school have been retained in the basement of the new building.

The school has been oriented to maximise the use of natural light. The building faces the shoreline but occupies a relatively sheltered position on this exposed coastline, tucked into the base of a steep hill. This position helps protect it from strong prevailing winds.

The entrance leads directly into the main communal hall linking the school and kindergarten. A loft area overlooks this space and is used as a platform, stage and a quiet place for group work. The school divides its pupils into two groups. Two classrooms provide a base for these groups, one for children aged 7 to 10 years and the other for those aged 11 to 13 years. A separate playroom is used by the kindergarten.

There are two outdoor areas. The lower area is a playground for the older children and for ball games. The higher area, outside the entrance, is softer surfaced and has a roof and walls on three sides. It provides shelter from gales and storms.

Above: *a playroom;*
Left: *the location;*
Below: *floor plan.*

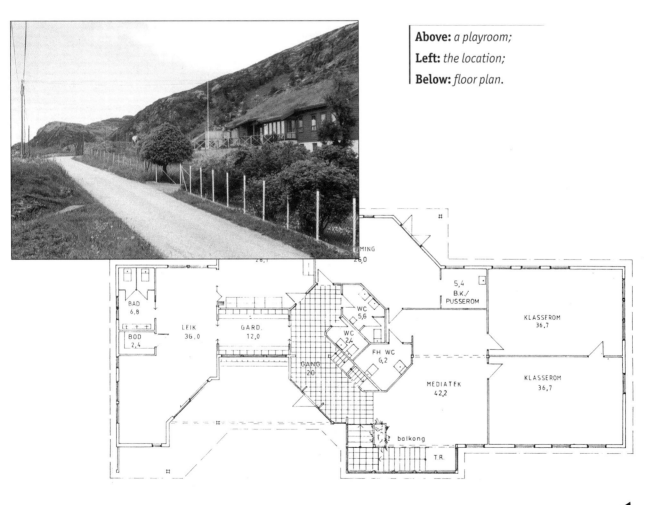

Schul-Haus-Boot Bertha von Suttner

Austria

ADDRESS	
	Donauinselplatz
	Vienna 21
	Austria

TELEPHONE
+43 1 271 4097

FAX
+43 1 271 6865

TYPE OF SCHOOL
secondary

NO. OF STUDENTS
1 000

AGE RANGE
10 to 18 years

TYPE OF PROJECT
new building

YEAR OF COMPLETION
1994

CLIENT
Federal Ministry of Education and Cultural Affairs

ARCHITECT
Bernhard Muller

Above: *the school's permanent mooring;*
Below: *view from across the Danube.*

At the beginning of the 1990s, the city of Vienna needed to set up new schools quickly to meet new demand caused in part by an influx of refugees from the former Yugoslavia. The authorities were faced with the challenge of finding available sites, financing land purchase and then building, within a few years, facilities for thousands of pupils.

An original and exemplary solution to this problem is a floating school. Set on the Danube river, Schul-Haus-Boot Bertha von Suttner is one example of this novel kind of school. Based in a purpose-built boat, it is made up of a number of pontoons that are closed ▶

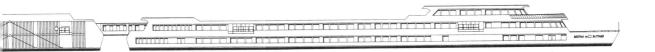

on all sides and linked by a covered way. There is full and safe access for the disabled with lifts connecting one level of the boat to another.

The internal organisation of the houseboat is based on existing space schedules for all schools. Spaces have been allocated for school administration, science, technical subjects, music, humanities and sports. The gym, work-out room and changing areas are located in a separate section to avoid disturbing classes in progress. The library is housed alongside a conservatory to provide a meeting space with quiet areas that can be used during study breaks.

Above: *elevation;*
Below: *first deck floor plan;* **Bottom:** *the access ramp.*

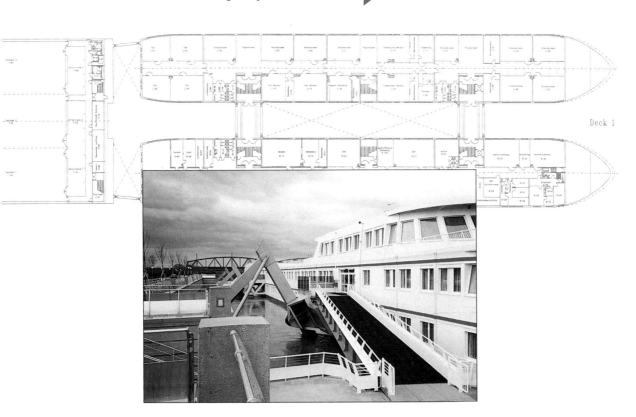

Deck 1

Built by the Korneuburg shipyard, the school-boats can be constructed within 22 months. Their specification respects all building regulations on land as well as those pertaining to ships. The total cost of the houseboat school is about a third less than that of an equivalent school built on land. Energy consumption is reduced by extracting heat from the Danube.

By setting schools on the Danube river, Vienna has solved the problem of finding suitable land for schools. The idea has attracted interest from several other education authorities.

Far left: *second deck floor plan;* **Left:** *a classroom;* **Below:** *the gymnasium.*

rural development

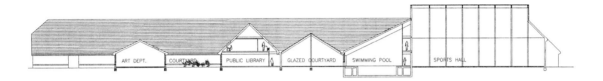

ART DEPT.   COURTYARD   PUBLIC LIBRARY   GLAZED COURTYARD   SWIMMING POOL   SPORTS HALL

This imaginative project has developed the traditional concept of a secondary school to provide a wide range of facilities for a remote, and relatively deprived, rural island community. The result is a successful amalgamation of educational, cultural, vocational, social and leisure services.

The new school is situated on the island of Benbecula. It is at the geographical centre of its catchment area, which includes neighbouring islands. It provides post-16 education, and as a result older pupils no longer need to leave home and board at the secondary school on the Isle of Lewis to continue their studies.

▶

Top: *view of school;*
Above: *east-west cross section.*

ADDRESS	
	Benbecula
Western Isles HS7 5PJ
United Kingdom
TELEPHONE	**+44 1870 602211**
FAX	**+44 1870 602817**
TYPE OF SCHOOL	**secondary**
NO. OF STUDENTS	**570**
AGE RANGE	**11 to 18 years**
TYPE OF PROJECT	**new building**
YEAR OF COMPLETION	**1988**
CLIENT	**Western Isles Island Council**
ARCHITECT	**John Patterson,
Director of Architectural Services**

◀ The building provides a focus for the whole community. In addition to the school, facilities include a public library, museum, swimming pool, sports hall, theatre, cafeteria, daycare centre, dental surgery and doctors' consulting room, and a hostel for 60 weekly boarders. The building is open from 9 a.m. to 9 p.m. and, where places are available, adults may attend the same classes as children.

The school has been designed to ensure that it withstands the rigours of an exposed coastal site. Particular attention has been paid to energy use. A compact building form helps to reduce energy consumption. Energy control measures include a building management system, low temperature underfloor heating, a 60 kW wind generator and a standby generator.

Above: *dining area;* **Top right:** *swimming pool;* **Right:** *ground floor plan.*

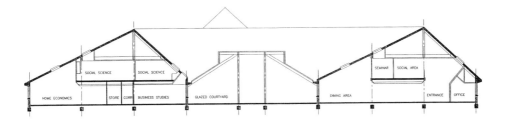

Top: *north-south cross section;* **Above left:** *public library;* **Above right:** *the theatre.*

Given the flat and exposed nature of the site, a traditional two-storey building was considered to be inappropriate. An innovative design locates academic areas within the roof space, lit by roof lights to the north and windows in re-entrant bays to the south. Two parallel wings link in three places to form sheltered courtyard areas, one of which has a glazed roof to create a wet weather recreation area.

Collège du Plan du Loup

France

ADDRESS
**63, chemin du Plan du Loup
69110 Sainte Foy les Lyon
France**

TELEPHONE
+33 72 16 70 90

FAX
+33 78 59 73 90

TYPE OF SCHOOL
lower secondary

NO. OF STUDENTS
653

AGE RANGE
12 to 16 years

TYPE OF PROJECT
new building

YEAR OF COMPLETION
1994

CLIENT
Rhône Departmental Council

ARCHITECT
Pierre Vurpas et associés

Set in the south-western suburbs of Lyon, this school caters for 550 pupils aged 12 to 16 in four academic levels and 100 pupils in special classes for those with learning difficulties. The new building replaces an old school that had become dilapidated and uncomfortable and, largely because of its metal structure, no longer met safety requirements.

The winning project in a competition organised by the Rhône Departmental Council, construction of the new ▶

Right: *in the atrium;*
Below: *south facade with main entrance (to left).*

school followed extensive public consultation and represents a strong response to the urban planning problems of the area. The aim was to create a modern facility where comfort and utility combine to form a pleasant working environment.

The school provides a new focus for the surrounding area. Its situation next to the old school building involved the replanning of the external areas. A footpath follows the access road as far as a

Below: *corridors linking the atrium with one of the wings;*
Right: *view of the atrium;*
Bottom: *floor plan.*

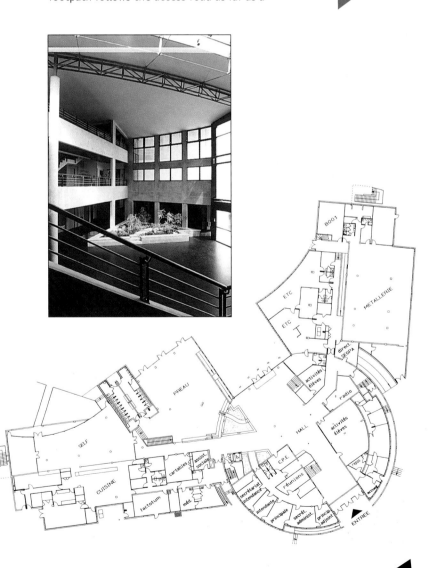

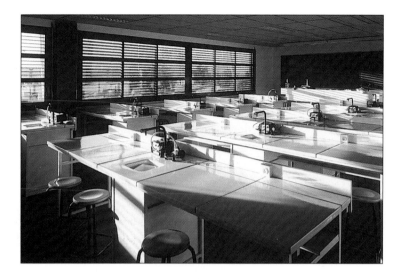

landscaped public square which becomes the focal point of the new site. The school forms the backdrop to the square. The new building has a strong architectural identity and dominates the site.

Functionally straightforward, the new school is easy to understand. The atrium, the heart of the building, marks both the transition between inside and outside and the crossroads for all the main internal circulation routes. A glass canopy runs from the entrance to the inner courtyard. Inside, all the services are located on two floors: reception, administration, documentation centre and common rooms for pupils and teachers.

Across the courtyard, and opening onto it, are the gymnasium and restaurant. The special education centre is also on ground level, in order to allow its pupils to join in easily with the life of the school. The main classrooms are located in the wings of the building on two levels linked by the atrium. Between the two wings lie the recreation area and the sports field.

Top: *science laboratory;*
Above: *the entrance hall;*
Below: *west elevation.*

onsite crèche

 Australia

Hobson's Bay Secondary College

The childcare centre at Hobson's Bay Secondary College is an autonomous unit, physically separated from the main building. Built as part of the A$ 3 million redevelopment of the college, it is the first public sector college-based daycare centre provided for teachers' children in the state of Victoria. The redevelopment also involved a complete renovation of the school as well as the construction of an A$ 1 million technology centre.

ADDRESS
88 Graham Street
Albert Park
Melbourne
Victoria 3206
Australia

TELEPHONE
+61 39 690 1633

FAX
+61 39 696 7169

TYPE OF SCHOOL
preschool, secondary, continuing education

NO. OF STUDENTS
crèche for 35 children

AGE RANGE
crèche for children up to 5 years
college for 11 to 19 years

TYPE OF PROJECT
adaptation and new building

YEAR OF COMPLETION
1992

CLIENT
Hobson's Bay Secondary College
School Council

ARCHITECT
Housing and Construction
Department, Victoria

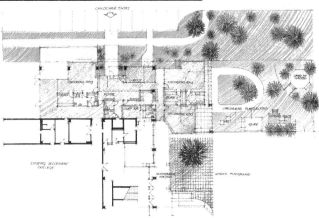

Above: *portico entrance to childcare centre;*
Left: *site plan.*

The centre provides care for children under the age of six years, for up to twelve hours a day. There is provision for 35 children in three rooms. The first room is a nursery for ten infants, the second room is available to ten children of 2 to 3 years, the third can accommodate fifteen 3 to 5 year-olds.

Designed to provide a space that feels like an extension of each child's family environment, the centre makes optimum use of the available natural light. This has been achieved by careful design of the ceiling profile and by using clerestory lighting and domelights.

As well as being used by teachers, the centre is also open to the local community, allowing women with young children to return to college or to continue their education. It is used in the evenings for professional development and during school holidays it offers a childcare facility for adults attending short courses.

Hobson's Bay Secondary College has become a unique educational setting; the school is linked with further education and provides adult education. The school also plays an important role in providing professional development to teachers, particularly in technology studies.

Institut Notre-Dame de Jupille

Belgium

Left: *renovated study room in original school;* **Below:** *elevation showing the three elements of the extended school.*

Set in a public park, the newly renovated and extended Institut of Notre-Dame has three elements. Complementing the original building, a new "cultural wing" has been built containing a library, dining room and activity rooms. Designed as a resource for ▶

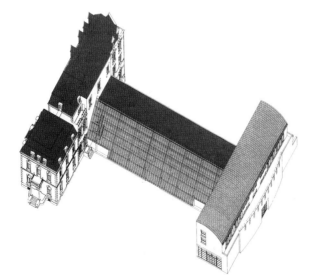

ADDRESS	
	47, rue Charlemagne
	4020 Jupille
	Liège
	Belgium
TELEPHONE	
FAX	
TYPE OF SCHOOL	secondary
NO. OF STUDENTS	670
AGE RANGE	12 to 18 years
TYPE OF PROJECT	reconstruction
YEAR OF COMPLETION	1993
CLIENT	Institut Notre-Dame de Jupille
ARCHITECT	Philippe Frere, l'arch' en ciel

◀ the school and the community, this new wing has a
separate entrance for public access. The third element
of the school is a dramatic glass "greenhouse" which
links the two main buildings.

The "greenhouse" has been designed to preserve as
far as possible the unity of the park. The effect of the
glass is to maintain the visual link between the two
sides of the park separated by the school buildings.
Yet it also provides the school with additional space.
There are a number of classrooms partly below ground ▶

Right: *ground floor plan;*
Below: *the old wing and
the new "greenhouse";*
Far right: *art class and
circulation route inside
the "greenhouse".*

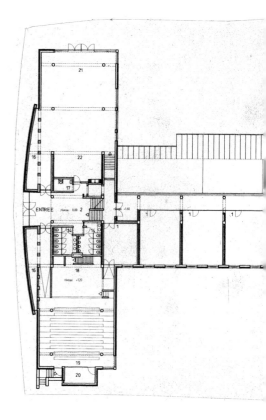

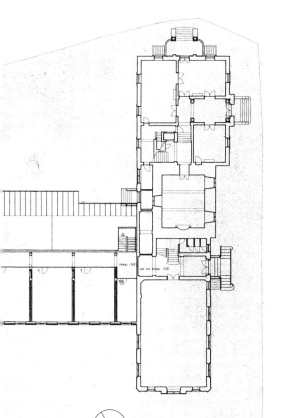

level which are lit by the glass canopy. At the upper level, there is a large and flexible space.

Although a striking building, the central "greenhouse" section was simple to build, uses reliable materials and is very easy to maintain. Both construction and recurrent maintenance costs are relatively low. With a load-bearing concrete frame, the internal partitions are easy to move and replace, so allowing considerable flexibility in the arrangement of the teaching areas.

Johan de Witt College

Netherlands

ADDRESS
Helena van Doeverenplantsoen 3
The Hague
Netherlands

TELEPHONE
+31 70 36 24 684

FAX
+31 70 36 03 076

TYPE OF SCHOOL
secondary,
vocational education

NO. OF STUDENTS
1 830

AGE RANGE
12 to 18 years

TYPE OF PROJECT
new building

YEAR OF COMPLETION
1991

CLIENT
Stichting Scholengemeenschap
Zuidwalland, The Hague

ARCHITECT
Campman, Tennekes, De Jong

Located in an area known for its many social problems, Johan de Witt College has been built alongside a small public park set among three- and four-storey housing. The original plan for a 20-storey building met with fierce local opposition. Following consultation on a new design, this initial resistance changed to constructive co-operation with the project. Now, the community is proud of the school.

The new school is housed in a three-storey building facing the park. On the ground floor, there is a large covered area which can be used as an auditorium and area for group activities. This is designed to compensate for the lack of a schoolyard. The classrooms are on the upper levels and are grouped around study areas for independent work. Lightwells bring daylight down to the centre of each floor. Sports facilities are situated above a public car park in a separate building across the street.

▶

Right: *view of school from across the park;* **Below:** *ground floor plan.*

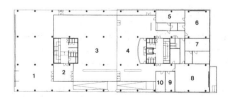

inner-city school

All photographs courtesy Michel Boesveld

In 1992, Johan de Witt won the Ministry of Education and Science's school building prize for its architectural design. Judges commended the clarity of the architectural concept and noted that the design succeeded in exploiting the site and town planning constraints to positive advantage. With 90 per cent of the student population of non-Dutch ethnic origin, the school has brought tangible benefits to the neighbourhood.

Above: *the school entrance;* **Below:** *cross section of building.*

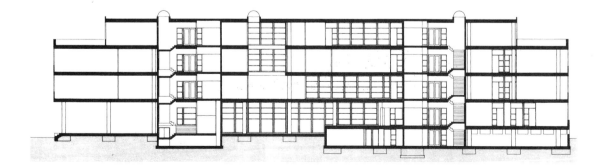

Vouliagmeni Gymnasion

Greece

| ADDRESS
Ektoros and L. Kavouriou Street
Vouliagmeni
Athens
Greece

| TELEPHONE
+30 1 9670 9678

| FAX

| TYPE OF SCHOOL
secondary

| NO. OF STUDENTS
270

| AGE RANGE
12 to 18 years

| TYPE OF PROJECT
new building

| YEAR OF COMPLETION
1994

| CLIENT
Municipality of Vouliagmeni

| ARCHITECT
Spelios Agiostratitis

The Secondary School of Vouliagmeni has been built in a 500-acre park purchased from the Greek Orthodox Church. It lies close to a public athletics centre. The design brief was to create an educational establishment that is integrated with the surrounding natural environment and that takes advantage of the nearby sports facilities.

The site is steeply sloping and quite heavily wooded, creating problems of access between the school and the athletics centre. However, the existing natural environment has been respected and all trees have been preserved. An interplay of walls define a variety of outdoor areas. There is a main school courtyard and easy access to the park.

Right (top to bottom):
school's setting; main entrance; sports facilities;
Below: *cross section.*

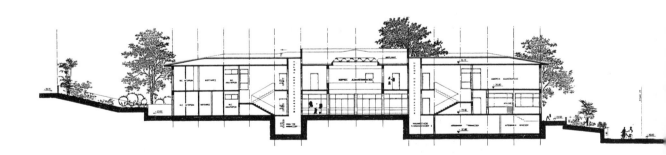

Visually, the school complements the surrounding residential district, which is predominantly low rise with steeply inclined tiled roofing. The architect has sought to project the school as an extension of the home. Typical domestic architectural features like arcades and verandas as well as the characteristic tiled roofs have been incorporated into the building.

Internal spaces are simple and are distributed symmetrically. The building is housed on two levels. Meeting rooms, laboratories and offices are on the ground floor and classrooms on the first floor.

Instituto de Educación Secundaria con Módulos Profesionales

Spain

ADDRESS
Pedrola
Zaragoza
Spain

TELEPHONE
+34 9 76 61 91 31

FAX
+34 9 76 61 91 82

TYPE OF SCHOOL
vocational education and training

NO. OF STUDENTS
750

AGE RANGE
12 to 20 years

TYPE OF PROJECT
new building

YEAR OF COMPLETION
1993

CLIENT
Ministry of Education

ARCHITECT
Javier Unceta Morales,
Antonio Cebrián García,
Joaquín Liart Camacho

All photographs courtesy Angel M Salcedo Oliver

Top: *view of school;*
Above: *elevations showing two facades.*

ALZADO SUR

SECCION TRANSVERSAL AA'

This centre is the result of a collaboration between the Spanish Ministry of Education and General Motors (Spain). With a nearby factory, the company is one of the major economic players in the central Ebro valley.

The centre provides secondary education and vocational training in electrical trades, electronics, automation, maintenance, administration and management. Some courses are held on General Motors' premises, while the centre also serves as a training centre for the company.

There are three main buildings; a school building, a workshop and a services building that includes a cafeteria and dining hall. The school building forms an H-shape. It is built on two levels, with teaching rooms radiating from a central lobby area. Each wing of the building accommodates a different discipline, and is formally and functionally independent. Noisier

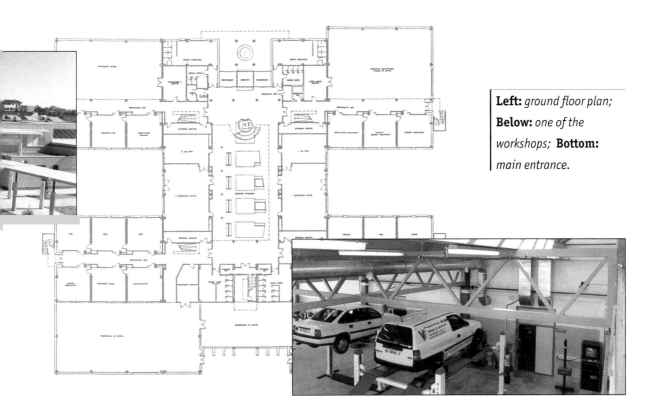

Left: *ground floor plan;*
Below: *one of the workshops;* **Bottom:** *main entrance.*

workshops are located on the outside and have separate external access.

A worthy expression of the new links existing between industry and education, the design breaks with the old idea of vocational education as a "second-class choice". Small communal lobby areas have been chosen in preference to corridors, circulation routes run along balconies rather than through enclosed corridors, and there is an abundance of natural light and greenery. The large double-height lobby is the architectural and social hub of the building.

Designed to be easily modified or extended, the centre has a simple and efficient layout, creating an effective and attractive whole. It has been built with a budget no greater than that of an average training centre.

Fukumitsu Lower Secondary School

 Japan

ADDRESS
720 Fukumitsu-machi,
Nishi-tonami-gun
Fukumitsu-machi,
Toyama
Japan

TELEPHONE
+81 763 52 1108

FAX

TYPE OF SCHOOL
lower secondary

NO. OF STUDENTS
395

AGE RANGE
13 to 15 years

TYPE OF PROJECT
new building

YEAR OF COMPLETION
1993

CLIENT
Fukumitsu Board of Education

ARCHITECT
Fukumi Architect and Associates

This new secondary school, completed in 1993, has been designed to be adaptable to changing educational needs. It seeks, in particular, to meet the community need for continuing education.

The way in which space is used in the school shows the special attention given to providing a welcoming environment for non-academic users. There are lounges and a hall where students and community users can meet, relax and study. These have been designed as an integral part of the site. Externally, the grounds have been landscaped with a pond and terrace to make them attractive.

Right: *main stairwell connecting floors.*

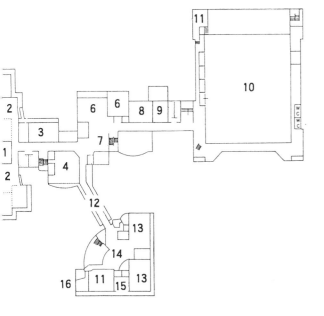

There are four main buildings; two accommodate the classrooms, one is a gymnasium and one is dedicated to arts subjects. In the main teaching blocks, there are several specialist rooms in addition to general purpose classrooms. As well as a language laboratory, there are rooms for computing, calligraphy, science, mathematics and English.

The arts block includes rooms for the secondary school, a community education centre and separate facilities for continuing education.

Top: *floor plan;* **Left:** *the school hall;* **Below:** *the landscaped grounds.*

Avonside Girls High School

New Zealand

ADDRESS
Avonside Drive
Christchurch 6
New Zealand

TELEPHONE
+64 3 3897 199

FAX
+64 3 3899 250

TYPE OF SCHOOL
secondary

NO. OF STUDENTS
1 033

AGE RANGE
13 to 18 years

TYPE OF PROJECT
renovation and extension

YEAR OF COMPLETION
1994

CLIENT
Ministry of Education

ARCHITECT
John Warren and Associates

Right: *main entrance with restored decorative parapets.*

Following the results of a 1986 feasibility study, a decision was taken not to demolish the existing Avonside Girls High School but to upgrade facilities and strengthen the old fabric to meet required earthquake standards. The project was undertaken as a single contract over three and a half years, but divided into three stages to allow continued use of two-thirds of the school buildings at any one time.

The original school building was constructed in 1927 and several extensions had been added over the next 26 years. As each was structurally quite different, it was necessary to design a strengthening system compatible with all the construction types.

▶

remodelling

The interior has been extensively remodelled to provide teaching spaces that fit new pedagogical models. A new central library has been built on the south side of the original 1927 section of the building. The materials used in this extension complement those of the existing walls. The school houses one computer suite on the upper level and allowance has been made for future cabling to connect different sites. The science laboratories have been modernised to promote the new science curriculum. The library, computer suite and science laboratories remain open during holidays for student and community use.

The original facade of the building has been retained, and decorative parapets removed in the 1960s because of earthquake risk have been reinstated using lightweight materials. Other historical parts of the building have been preserved, as well as existing doors, fixed lights, staircases and balustrades, and column and beam structures.

Partitioning installed over the years has been removed, opening up the original volume. Space has been regained so that pupils are able to move through foyers and along wide carpeted corridors. There is a sense of calm in the building, even at busy times, with views across the open space and out to the trees and river.

Above: *the library;*
Below: *ground floor plan.*

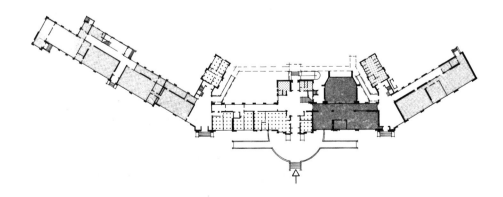

Instituto Claudio Moyano

Spain

| ADDRESS
Zamora
Spain

| TELEPHONE
+34 9 80 52 04 00

| FAX
+34 9 80 51 21 54

| TYPE OF SCHOOL
secondary

| NO. OF STUDENTS
1 000

| AGE RANGE
14 to 18 years

| TYPE OF PROJECT
renovation

| YEAR OF COMPLETION
1992

| CLIENT
Ministry of Education

| ARCHITECT
Pedro Lucas del Teso,
Jesús Perucho Lezcano,
Leandro Iglesias Lorenzo

This historic school, designed by Miguel Mathet, was built in the early years of this century. The architectural and ornamental richness of the building reflected the educational ideals of the period. Built in brick on two levels, the original school had a quadrangular form and surrounded a central courtyard. However, after 80 years, the building had physically deteriorated, it lacked sufficient large spaces and was no longer suitable for teaching.

Below left: *aerial view;*
Below right: *ground floor plan.*

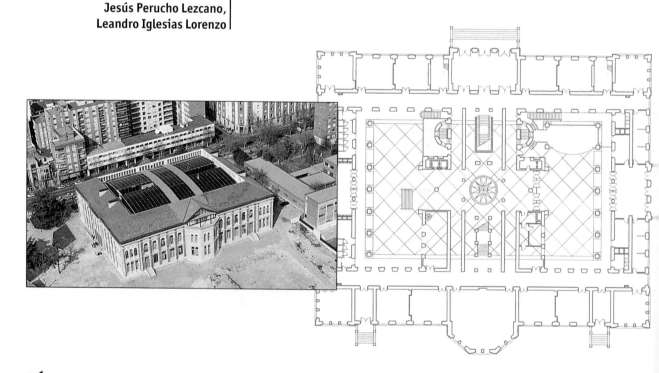

Above: *the external facade.*

The renovation aimed to create a modern teaching facility yet retain the character of the original building. The most significant feature of the project has been the covering of the courtyard. This has created space for the main entrance hall as well as a large multipurpose hall and theatre. A new central staircase has been built. This work has expanded the floor area of the school by 85 per cent without changing the volume of the building or going beyond its original perimeter.

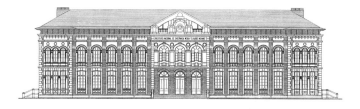

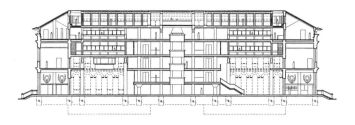

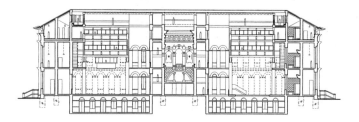

Top: *detail of new roof covering courtyard;* **Above right:** *central staircase;* **Above left:** *elevation and cross sections.*

With a capacity for 1 000 pupils in compulsory secondary education and vocational training, the renovated Claudio Moyano Institute has four floors. The project demonstrates a genuine revitalisation of a building that had been ill-suited to today's educational requirements. Now a superb teaching facility, the richness of the original has been preserved and is complemented by the modern extension.

Above: *part of the covered courtyard.*

Istituto Tecnico Commerciale Marco Polo

Italy

| ADDRESS
**via Mons. Ruggero Bovelli 3
44100 Ferrara
Italy**

| TELEPHONE
+39 532 209 346

| FAX
+39 532 202 365

| TYPE OF SCHOOL
vocational education

| NO. OF STUDENTS
460

| AGE RANGE
14 to 19 years

| TYPE OF PROJECT
renovation

| YEAR OF COMPLETION
1993

| CLIENT
Province of Ferrara

| ARCHITECT
**Davide Rubbini and
Stefano Marini, UTECO**

Built in 1515 and expanded during the Renaissance, the former Dominican convent of Santa Monica retained its pristine features until the early twentieth century. Between 1920 and 1960, the building lost much of its architectural unity in a series of additions and alterations to house two secondary schools and a gymnasium.

Right: *the convent before restoration;* **Below:** *the restored convent building;* **Left:** *first floor plan.*

converted convent

In the 1990s, it was decided to house the Marco Polo School in the former convent. As well as accommodating the school, the aim was to conserve an important part of the town's architectural heritage and to provide a building for community use. The project is regarded as an example of integrated conservation, comprising both restoration techniques and attempts to define community functions.

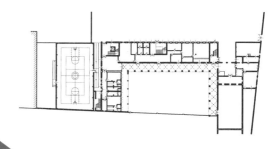

Top right: *ground floor plan;* **Right:** *the cloisters.*

Right: *the auditorium before restoration;* **Bottom:** *the restored building with original wood beams;* **Centre:** *the cloister arcade.*

The renovation of this historical site to meet the contemporary needs of a technical and foreign language high school has entailed a series of sophisticated architectural operations, from the detailed scientific restoration of the original frescos of the former choir to the complete reconstruction of some sections of the building.

converted convent

Left: *the gymnasium;*
Centre: *cloisters at night;*
Bottom: *computer room.*

The school comprises 20 classrooms, laboratories, a
library, a printing shop, administration offices, an
auditorium and sports facilities. Great imagination
has been devoted to the renovation and the practical
integration of the high school's different sections.
The main wing has been converted into classrooms,
the area around the cloisters transformed into a
library and the choir itself is used as a meeting room.
The former rooms on the upper level have been
altered to form scientific and business areas.

Lycée La Fayette

France

| ADDRESS
21, boulevard Robert Schuman
63002 Clermont-Ferrand
Cedex 01
France|

| TELEPHONE
+33 73 28 08 08 |

| FAX
+33 73 28 08 42 |

| TYPE OF SCHOOL
upper secondary |

| NO. OF STUDENTS
1 480 |

| AGE RANGE
15 to 22 years |

| TYPE OF PROJECT
new building |

| YEAR OF COMPLETION
1991 |

| CLIENT
Auvergne Regional Council |

| ARCHITECT
Christian Hauvette |

Replacing the celebrated Amadée Gasquet Technical College which closed after 70 years' service, the Lycée La Fayette is devoted to scientific education. Students prepare for the scientific baccalaureate, technical baccalaureates in mechanics, electronics and civil engineering or for technical qualifications for entry to France's *grandes écoles* (university-level engineering schools).

Right: *exterior view of main elliptical building.*

Left: *aerial view of the lycée;* **Below:** *facade of the main building.*

The main part of the building is elliptical in shape and has similar dimensions to the Roman arena at Nîmes. It consists of two concentric ellipses, four storeys high, with the inner ellipse leaning on the outer one at third-floor level. Circulation space is provided by walkways running round the two ellipses.

The technology laboratories, kitchens and a restaurant are housed in a separate rectangular building which is tangential to the main building. A group of smaller pavilions provide boarding accommodation for students and staff. The cascade of windows on the inner facade of the ellipse encircles the courtyard and the combination of glass, aluminium and concrete echoes the colours of the local Volvic stone.

Efforts have been made to use energy effectively and to control energy costs. The number and variety of buildings and the fluctuating patterns of usage makes energy management complex. A highly sophisticated natural gas system is based on two main boiler houses with separate boilers in each of the nine pavilions. The whole system is managed from a central control room. The additional cost of the equipment is expected to be recouped over a relatively short payback period through lower energy bills.

Below: *bird's-eye view of campus;* **Right:** *an interior walkway;* **Below right:** *the courtyard.*

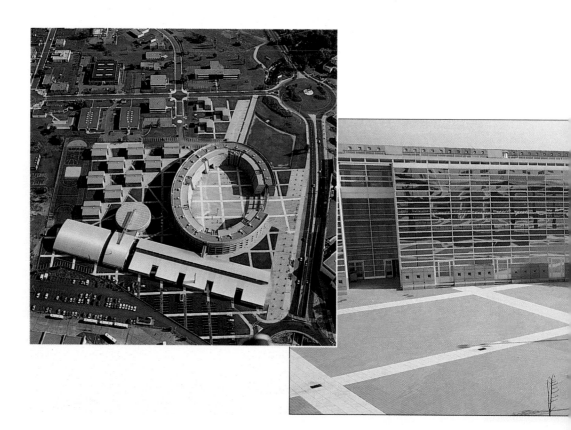

Chapmanskolan

Sweden

All photographs courtesy Nils-Erik Larsson

ADDRESS	
	Box 309
	S-37125 Karlskrona
	Sweden

TELEPHONE
+46 455 76054

FAX
+46 455 76059

TYPE OF SCHOOL
upper secondary

NO. OF STUDENTS
2 400

AGE RANGE
16 to 19 years

TYPE OF PROJECT
renovation and extension

YEAR OF COMPLETION
1991

CLIENT
Karlskrona Municipality

ARCHITECT
White Arkitekter AB

Chapmanskolan is located in the centre of Karlskrona's administrative, cultural and commercial district. It is housed in a number of buildings in and around the former town hall. Built in 1750, the town hall became a grammar school in 1825. In 1877, neighbouring buildings were purchased from a distillery company. A gymnasium was added in the 1930s.

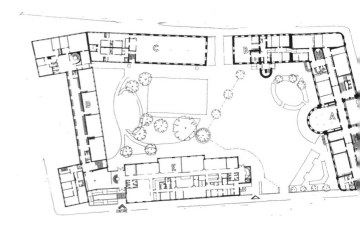

Above: *site plan;* **Right:** *view across courtyard to the old school building.*

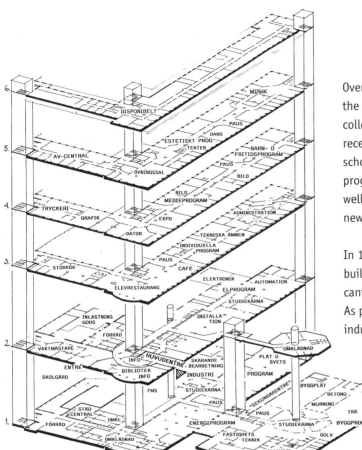

Over the years, educational usage has changed. First, the site was developed to accommodate a technical college and then a technical high school. More recently, it has been adapted to teach the senior high school curricula. This has required a major renovation programme to meet changing educational needs as well as the acquisition of further buildings and some new construction.

In 1984, the municipality took over a number of buildings from the Navy. The former dining hall and canteen building were converted to educational use. As pupil numbers continued to grow, a large industrial telecommunications property adjoining the

Above: *floor plan of the science and information technology block;*
Left: *assembly hall in the former town hall.*

school was acquired. Chapmanskolan took possession of the site in 1994.

During the 1980s, the old technical college was completely renovated. The adaptation of the former town hall was completed in 1991. It now houses a number of well-equipped facilities for teaching subjects in the humanities, and social, natural and economic sciences, as well as two assembly halls. Science and information technology rooms are accommodated in another renovated and converted building which adjoins a new block housing the school restaurant and cafeteria, the principal's office and some general classrooms.

The whole school is now complete and all premises are equipped to modern standards. There is a library, five information technology centres with rooms for group activities, and sports facilities. A broadband network provides state-of-the-art technology for educational, administrative and library use.

Above: *student in the automation workshop;* **Below:** *multimedia workstation;* **Bottom:** *the library.*

Lugnetgymnasiet, Mediehuset

Sweden

Famous for graphic art, the town of Falun has strong ties with the media industry. Swedish state television, regional radio and educational radio have production studios in the town. Falun also houses the editorial offices of two newspapers, some 25 graphic design companies and an educational video company. These links with the media have been strengthened by the opening in 1993 of a purpose-built institute to provide education and training in media production. ▶

ADDRESS	Lugnetsvägen 3 S-79131 Falun Sweden
TELEPHONE	+46 23 83460
FAX	+46 23 83847
TYPE OF SCHOOL	vocational education (media studies)
NO. OF STUDENTS	1 200
AGE RANGE	16 to 19 years
TYPE OF PROJECT	new construction
YEAR OF COMPLETION	1993
CLIENT	Falun Municipality
ARCHITECT	Skanska AB

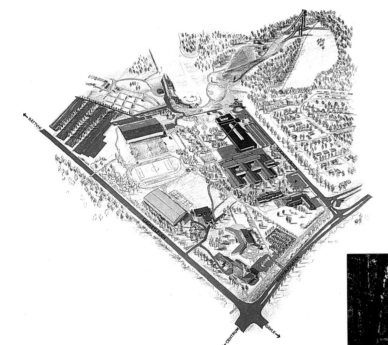

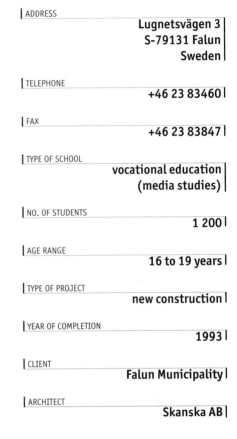

Above: *site plan, the Media House (B) is situated next to the secondary school (A);*
Right: *view of Media House from the school.*

The Media House is a co-operative venture between Lugnet Upper Secondary School, Falun Institute of Adult Education, the University of Falun and Borlänge, and the State Vocational Training School. It provides a comprehensive three-year media education for high school students as well as a technologically advanced resource for the university and adult education.

Below left: *foyer;* **Below right:** *the Media House's film and television studio.*

The need to accommodate studios and darkrooms – that have particular requirements for sound proofing and air humidity – influenced the choice of building material and construction. Outer walls are concrete, with curtain walls of timber clad with wood panels, bricks and sheeting. The inner walls consist of gypsum wallboard finished with painted woven fabric.

Designed and organised to cater for a wide variety of disciplines within the media production industry, the Media House has the facilities to teach photography, film and video production, sound recording, printing and bookbinding.

factory conversion

Randaberg videregående skole

Norway

Occupying the site of a former printing works, Randaberg upper secondary school runs general and business studies programmes, foundation and advanced courses for a range of industrial and professional trades, and some apprenticeship training programmes.

In developing the site, the project team faced the challenge of converting the square colossus of the factory into an educational institution. The main architectural features of the exterior have largely been retained. The exterior brown corrugated steel cladding has been replaced with new white cladding. Two new entrances for students have been constructed with the original main entrance retained as the administration entrance. New canopies have been added above the entrances and the surroundings have been landscaped.

Inside, new floors have been constructed. The large interior volume of the building has been opened by ▶

ADDRESS	Grødemsveien 70 N-4070 Randaberg Norway
TELEPHONE	+47 51 41 55 00
FAX	+47 51 41 04 99
TYPE OF SCHOOL	upper secondary
NO. OF STUDENTS	800
AGE RANGE	16 to 19 years
TYPE OF PROJECT	renovation and extension
YEAR OF COMPLETION	1984
CLIENT	Randaberg Municipality
ARCHITECT	Helliesen, Wåge and Hallgren

Left: *the renovated factory exterior with new student entrances.*

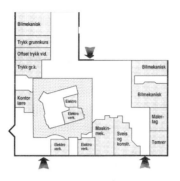 

two large roof lights (each 7 m. by 50 m.) situated above walkways. The walkways function as main communication routes, allowing ease of access between different teaching rooms and recreation areas. Classrooms face onto an interior courtyard. The library is located in the centre of the building and is easy to reach from all parts of the school.

As well as finding a good use for a redundant factory, the project made substantial savings in time and money for the municipal authorities. Cheaper than building a new school of comparable capacity, the project took less than two years from developing the initial concept to completing the conversion.

Above: *ground and first floor plans;* **Below:** *part of the interior courtyard.*

business class

ADDRESS	
	Vejlby Centervej 50
	DK-8240 Risskov
	Denmark

TELEPHONE	
	+45 89 363800

FAX	
	+45 89 363808

TYPE OF SCHOOL	
	vocational education
	(business)

NO. OF STUDENTS	
	800

AGE RANGE	
	16 to 20 years

TYPE OF PROJECT	
	new building

YEAR OF COMPLETION	
	1993

CLIENT	
	Århus Business College

ARCHITECT	
	Kjaer & Richter

Above: *administration building;* **Left:** *view from the water garden.*

Århus Købmandsskole is a new business college for vocational education and training in northern Denmark. The aim of the project was to provide a stimulating learning environment. By allowing flexible use of available space, it was also the intention to achieve a high level of space utilisation.

Right: *central assembly hall and canteen;*
Middle: *floor plan.*

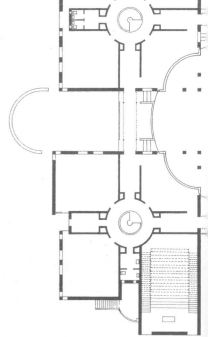

All photographs courtesy Thomas Pederson and Poul Pederson

Six independent buildings have been placed close to one another. Four of them intersect at four corners, forming a unified whole comprising the assembly hall and canteen. Functionally, the school is divided into three units, two with classrooms and areas for group projects, the third being occupied by the staff facilities, school administration and computer rooms.

A good balance has been achieved between the distribution of spaces for classrooms, individual student work, teamwork activities and the areas for

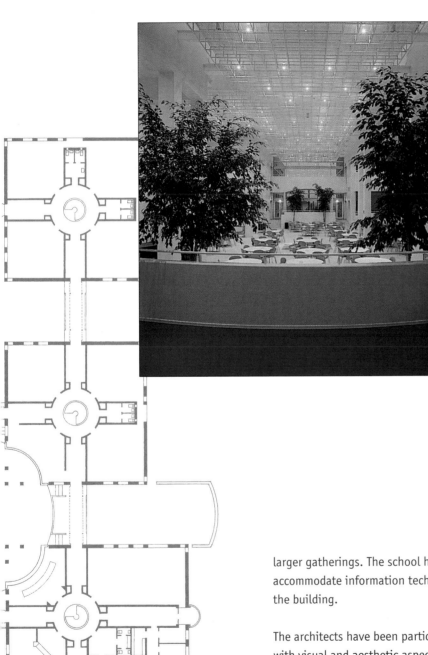

Left: *another view of central assembly hall.*

larger gatherings. The school has been designed to accommodate information technology throughout the building.

The architects have been particularly concerned with visual and aesthetic aspects, making extensive use of natural and artificial light and working out the building elements in human proportions. Natural materials and an efficient ventilation system make for a comfortable indoor climate.

Above: *exit from assembly hall;* **Below:** *view of college.*

◀ Care has been taken to make the college grounds attractive for students and staff. The buildings are surrounded by a park, planted with small oak trees, flowering trees and bushes. There is a water garden to the west and planted gardens to the north and south.

Ecole et stations agricoles cantonales de Grange-Verney

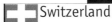Switzerland

Agriculture is undergoing profound change. Technical requirements are constantly evolving. Farming methods are becoming more complex, agricultural tools and machinery are increasingly sophisticated.

▶

ADDRESS	1510 Moudon Vaud Switzerland
TELEPHONE	+41 21 995 34 34
FAX	+41 21 995 34 30
TYPE OF SCHOOL	vocational training, continuing education
NO. OF STUDENTS	172
AGE RANGE	16 to 20 years
TYPE OF PROJECT	new building
YEAR OF COMPLETION	1994-95
CLIENT	Canton of Vaud, Buildings Department
ARCHITECT	Laurent Faessler and Ines Werner

Above: *workshop building within the complex of farm buildings;* **Right:** *site plan.*

Right: *walkway across fields to the workshops;*
Below: *a workshop;*
Bottom: *detail of facade.*

Farmers need information and vocational training to keep up to date. By providing bridges between different farming occupations, agricultural schools can help those farmers wishing to diversify and ensure that farming practices complement one another more fully.

This school is sited in a rural district, away from urban and industrial areas. It aims to make a significant contribution to the local agricultural economy. The school buildings form two distinct groupings; the administrative and teaching blocks are close to the main road, and the farm buildings located by the edge of the forest. The project sought to unify these two elements.

The site comprises a teaching block, a workshop building for mechanical engineering, welding and woodwork together with boarding accommodation. There is also a cafeteria, meeting rooms, laboratory and offices for agricultural associations. The buildings make extensive use of timber, both in the structural frame and in the floors, internal partitions and cladding.

The facility is designed to cater for a wide variety of students. It provides vocational training (with boarding accommodation) for young people, courses and workshops for practising farmers, and seminars for professional groups. It provides a focus for farmers from across the district to exchange experience and to study new farming techniques.

individualised learning

Left: *ground floor plan;* **Below:** *southern aspect.*

ADDRESS	Tryggvagötu IS-800 Selfoss Iceland
TELEPHONE	+354 482 2111
FAX	
TYPE OF SCHOOL	upper secondary
NO. OF STUDENTS	650
AGE RANGE	16 to 20 years and above
TYPE OF PROJECT	new building
YEAR OF COMPLETION	1994
CLIENT	Selfoss Town
ARCHITECT	Maggi Jónsson

Fjölbrautarskóli is a regional upper secondary comprehensive school. It is located in Selfoss, a town of just over 4 000 inhabitants, but attracts pupils from a wide rural catchment area of about 16 000 people. It was built in two phases, opening in 1987 and 1994 respectively.

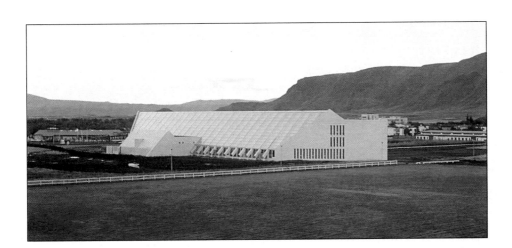

Above: *school and main entrance;* **Right:** *looking down into the common area;* **Below:** *lateral cross section.*

The school operates on the unit-credit system. Pupils select a programme of study, comprising a number of individual courses or credits. In this system, each pupil has a personal timetable and graduates from a particular course when he or she has completed the required number of credits.

In designing the school building, the aim was to foster cohesion and an identification with the school among students pursuing widely different programmes of study. In addition, as substantial

numbers of pupils commute daily to the school in school buses, it was necessary to provide areas for students to relax and study during the free periods in their schedules.

These factors led to the adoption of a centralised design. A spacious, glass-roofed common area with a southern exposure has created a variety of spaces. These balconies, nooks and corners, together with a cafeteria, allow pupils to meet between lessons, rest and form social connections. It is widely used and popular with students.

▶

Left: *walkways and stairs down to the common area;* **Below:** *east-west elevation.*

Above: *classroom;*
Below: *technical drawing studio.*

Since the school opened, a significantly greater proportion of local young people have entered upper secondary education. The school has attracted hundreds of visitors from abroad.

applied science

Situated in the eastern suburbs of Orléans, the lycée in St-Jean-de-Braye is named after the Nobel Prize-winning scientist Jacques Monod. It is a general and technical secondary school specialising in physics and chemistry and their industrial applications. The 27 000 sq. m. building was completed in 1989.

The architecture seeks to express the scientific vocation of the school through both its shape and its colour. The buildings display both daring and harmony, integrating well with the various new buildings that make up the town centre of St-Jean-de-Braye.

ADDRESS
**rue Léon Blum
48503 St-Jean-de-Braye
France**

TELEPHONE
+33 38 55 68 69

FAX
+33 38 61 58 00

TYPE OF SCHOOL
upper secondary

NO. OF STUDENTS
1 336

AGE RANGE
16 to 20 years

TYPE OF PROJECT
new building

YEAR OF COMPLETION
1989

CLIENT
Centre Regional Council

ARCHITECT
Costantini Regembal Lemaire

Far left: *glass-covered utility area;* **Left:** *science laboratory.*

Two main elements of the institution, the teaching accommodation and the boarding facilities, are separated by a public thoroughfare. The two buildings are linked by a footbridge. The school itself houses an open-air amphitheatre and a large glassed-in area which can serve as a setting for concerts.

The lycée is designed to make a positive contribution to urban renewal. It is situated in close proximity to the sports hall, a supermarket, the bus station and a number of other buildings housing public services and shops.

Above: *the teaching block (left) is linked to the administration block by an aerial walkway;* **Below:** *school buildings across the courtyard.*

shipyard conversion

Turku Music Conservatory

 Finland

ADDRESS	
	Linnankatu 60
	SF-20100 Turku
	Finland

TELEPHONE
+358 21 2507600

FAX
+358 21 2535610

TYPE OF SCHOOL
music school

NO. OF STUDENTS
976

AGE RANGE
1 to 30 years

TYPE OF PROJECT
adaptation and renovation

YEAR OF COMPLETION
1994

CLIENT
Turku and
surrounding districts

ARCHITECT
Laiho, Pulkkinen,
Raunio Architects

Top: *elevation of one of the shipbuilding halls;*
Above: *recital room;*
Right: *part of the site before renovation.*

In 1987, the City of Turku organised an architectural competition to produce a master plan for the redevelopment of the west bank of the river Aura. The winning entry proposed transforming this former shipbuilding area by adapting the existing industrial buildings for educational purposes and by creating a museum and offices.

Left: *entrance to adapted shipbuilding hall;*
Below: *elevation showing internal detail.*

Two massive shipbuilding halls and a former rope factory will house a major fine arts complex. The music conservatory, completed in 1994, is housed in one of these halls. It also occupies the major part of the rope factory. The second hall will house the Turku School of Art and Communication. Turku School of Fine Arts is already located in the same block. It is eventually planned to link all three schools by using the rope factory's "chute" as a connecting corridor.

Within the conservatory complex, efforts have been made to preserve the original sense of space. Classrooms and practice facilities are located on two levels in the former rope factory, where the ordered spacing of the windows allows for a natural division into rooms. Administration and offices for teachers are located in the "chute" area. A small space between the rope factory and the shipbuilding hall

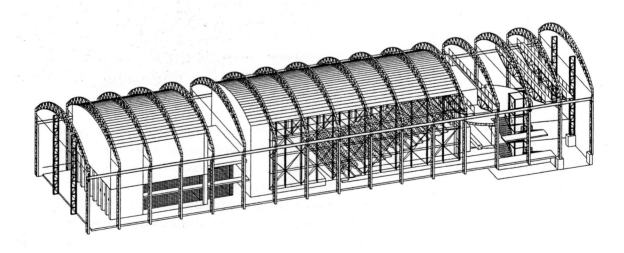

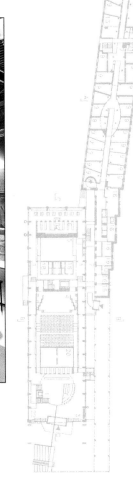

Above: *classroom;*
Left: *first floor plan;*
Right: *ground floor plan.*

◀ has been covered with glass and is used as an entry space to both buildings.

In the former shipbuilding hall, the high ceiling guarantees an ideal environment for music teaching. The hall accommodates a 400-seat auditorium, together with recital rooms and a music library. These spaces have been created as new and separate structures within the original building. The auditorium walls are constructed of glass, extending space visually to the older, outer walls. This has been done to minimise noise pollution from the street, and to protect the existing, riveted steel, exterior wall structures.

Externally, the buildings are largely unchanged. Inside, load-bearing structures such as moving bridge cranes have been preserved and utilised wherever possible.

Centre de formation en alimentation et tourisme

 Canada

ADDRESS
164 rue Wellington Nord
Sherbrooke
Québec J1H 5C5
Canada

TELEPHONE
+1 819 822 5361

FAX
+1 819 822 6879

TYPE OF SCHOOL
vocational education
and training

NO. OF STUDENTS
200

AGE RANGE
16 years and above

TYPE OF PROJECT
adaptation and extension
of an existing building

YEAR OF COMPLETION
1996

CLIENT
Sherbrooke Catholic
Schools' Board

ARCHITECT
Jubinville et Mailhot

The building which now houses this centre for catering and tourism was originally an ironmongery store. Of considerable architectural interest, the four-storey building has some 800 sq. m. of floor space on each level. When acquired by the municipal authorities, it was in excellent structural condition.

The centre was located on this site as part of a broader plan to revitalise the city centre. The challenge was to adapt the building to incorporate three teaching kitchens, a dining room, a storeroom and a bakery together with classrooms and staff rooms. This required extending the original building, both onto the adjacent site where a neighbouring building was demolished and behind the next building further down the street.

▶

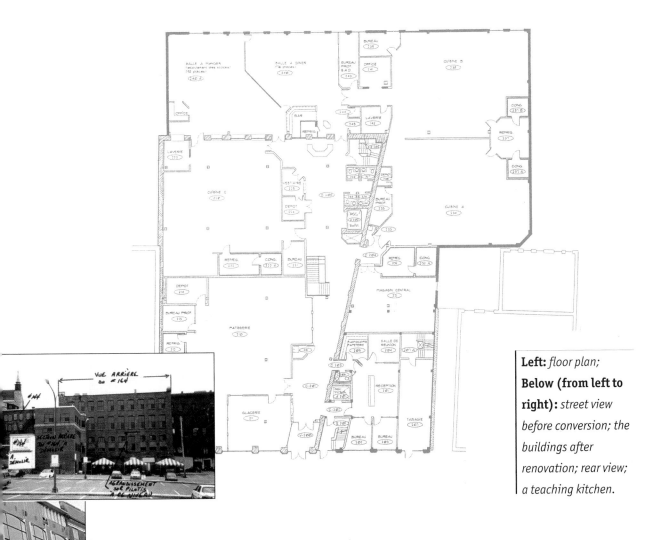

Left: *floor plan;*
Below (from left to right): *street view before conversion; the buildings after renovation; rear view; a teaching kitchen.*

At street level (level two), there are the teaching kitchens, dining room and bakery. Butchery is taught in the basement. The other classrooms and staff rooms are on the third level, while the upper level houses the ventilation and central heating plant. There is some unused space which could be fitted out in the future to provide more teaching and workshop space.

Surrounded by shops and other businesses, the training centre integrates well with the other commercial activities in the area.

Coffs Harbour Education Campus
Australia

ADDRESS

Hogbin Drive
Coffs Harbour
NSW 2450
Australia

TELEPHONE

+61 66 593000

FAX

+61 66 593071

TYPE OF SCHOOL

upper secondary,
vocational training,
higher education

NO. OF STUDENTS

2 500

AGE RANGE

16 years and above

TYPE OF PROJECT

new building

YEAR OF COMPLETION

1995

CLIENT

Coffs Harbour City Council,
Ministry of Education,
Department of School Education,
TAFE Commission,
Southern Cross University

ARCHITECT

NSW State Projects
with Conrad and
Gargett Architects

Above: *aerial view of campus;* **Right:** *view from within the central assembly area;* **Far Right:** *exterior views of buildings and site plan.*

Coffs Harbour Education Campus is an integrated facility combining a university, a TAFE (Technical and Further Education) college and a senior high school. The campus breaks new ground in the articulation of the curriculum, educational administration and facility design, eliminating traditional divisions between educational institutions. The physical integration of the institutions enables students to choose flexible pathways across courses.

Located on a narrow coastal strip sandwiched between the Pacific Ocean and an escarpment, Coffs

Harbour is an innovative built environment. The campus has been designed to minimise the impact on the natural environment while incorporating latest technology and design. A conscious effort was made

to maintain significant landscape features and accentuate these by the buildings. A minimal amount of vegetation has been removed and rainwater site run-off is controlled to avoid contaminating the surrounding wetlands.

The design criteria emphasised the need for an energy-efficient environment with low maintenance costs. The campus incorporates principles of passive solar design, with effective insulation, air conditioning and heat recovery. The buildings are designed to make the best use of daylight. Radiating

from a central, circular assembly area, buildings are oriented to take advantage of prevailing breezes to maximise natural ventilation.

The project has aimed to set benchmarks in areas such as communications and information technology, access management and security. The communications system allows interactive distance learning and encourages industry participation. Movement across the campus is through a network of colonnades and covered walkways. All facilities are fully accessible to people with disabilities.

Open Training and Education Network
Australia

ADDRESS	
	51 Wentworth Road
	Strathfield
	NSW 2135
	Australia

TELEPHONE	
	+61 2 715 8000

FAX	
	+61 2 715 8111

TYPE OF SCHOOL	
	distance and open learning,
	secondary, vocational education

NO. OF STUDENTS	
	more than 28 000

AGE RANGE	
	16 years and above

TYPE OF PROJECT	
	new building

YEAR OF COMPLETION	
	1995

CLIENT	
	Department of School Education and
	TAFE Commission, New South Wales

ARCHITECT	
	Philip Cox

Above and right: *the main entrance;* **Far right:** *site plan of the complex.*

Open and distance education exploits new information and communication technologies for learning. Although their learning involves fewer structured situations, students do need access to educational facilities. Open learning institutions need to provide study and work space, meeting rooms for tutorials, and the institutions themselves need facilities such as laboratories, libraries, studios and specialised equipment rooms.

This purpose-built complex, designed by Philip Cox for the Open Training and Education Network, is a response to the changing methods and technologies used to deliver open and distance learning. It is the main support facility for distance and open learning programmes in the state of New South Wales.

▶

The new structure integrates two existing buildings with a series of three-storey office wings to form a complex around a central open courtyard. A single-storey pavilion leading to a double-height circulation spine provides the main entry point and organisation for the facility. A communications tower situated at the joint of this pavilion and circulation spine serves both a functional and symbolic role, signalling the high-tech communications work of the facility.

In most of the complex, offices are open plan and there is space for the production of learning materials. The complex houses an administration unit, offices for teaching and support staff, a

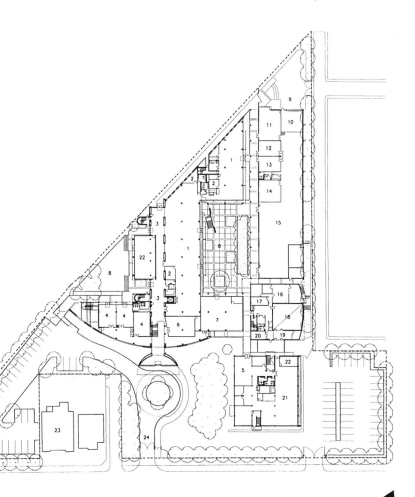

television and film studio, and a learning materials distribution centre which includes a warehousing operation. It also accommodates three seminar rooms, a library and video centre, an educational technology and systems area and a business centre available for public hire.

Left: *looking out to central courtyard;* **Right:** *main circulation spine.*

The infrastructure of the new building has been designed to provide an "integrated technology platform", enabling the institute's four computing systems to talk to one another. The aim is to provide a flexible communication backbone to support open and distance learning. Staff access E-mail, bulletin boards and conferencing facilities on a common linkup and students have 24-hour access to open learning resources and video conferencing facilities.

Ecole des métiers et occupations de l'industrie de la construction de Québec

Canada

The creation of this new education and training centre for the building trades was achieved through the extensive renovation of an existing building and the construction of a modern extension. The new centre can accommodate more than 500 students as well as 60 teaching and non-teaching staff.

Training workshops in a school of this type are indoor building sites. So, in drawing up plans for the centre, there has been an emphasis on health and safety. Some parts of the existing building have been demolished because they could not meet

ADDRESS
1060, rue Borne
Québec G1N 2L9
Canada

TELEPHONE
+1 418 681 3512

FAX
+1 418 681 2410

TYPE OF SCHOOL
vocational education,
adult education

NO. OF STUDENTS
478

AGE RANGE
17 years and above

TYPE OF PROJECT
renovation and extension

YEAR OF COMPLETION
1994

CLIENT
Québec Catholic Schools' Board

ARCHITECT
Beaudet & Nolet,
Régis Coté et associés

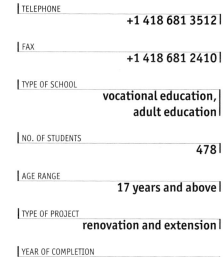

Above: *corridor leading to first-floor workshops;*
Right: *street view.*

Right: *main entrance;*
Below: *entrance hall;*
Bottom: *site plan.*

environmental and safety standards. The areas that were retained have been enlarged and reorganised.

Careful thought has been given to the layout to ensure effective utilisation of space. Workshops requiring heavy equipment – carpentry and joinery, bricklaying and stonemasonry, and the preparation and working of concrete – have been located on the ground floor. Workshops using lighter equipment, for example those for painting and decorating, electrical systems and plastering, are on the first floor. Classrooms are also on the first floor. To ensure flexibility, the workshops on the ground floor have been built over a crawl space so that it is easy to install and reroute drains, pipes and cables.

By constructing a circulation route between the new extension and the renovated building, the architects have created a space for the main entrance hall and a common area for students, allowing people on different courses somewhere to mix and relax.

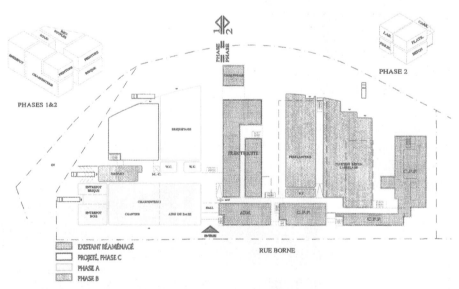

Escola Marquesa de Alorna, Resource Centre

Portugal

New legislation in Portugal has made it a requirement that schools have educational resource centres. Built in 1959, the Marquesa de Alorna Primary School chose to create a resource centre by adapting some of the original classrooms.

The classrooms have been remodelled to provide access to a range of teaching and communication technologies, including personal computers, television and other audio-visual media. There is a darkroom, graphic design studio, audio-visual production suite and study rooms.

As well as a resource for the primary school, the centre serves neighbouring schools and the wider ▶

ADDRESS	rua Dr Júlio Dantas 1300 Lisbon Portugal
TELEPHONE	+351 1 387 0992/3
FAX	+351 1 387 3102
TYPE OF SCHOOL	learning resource centre in a primary school, teacher training
NO. OF STUDENTS	not applicable
AGE RANGE	all ages
TYPE OF PROJECT	renovation and adaptation
YEAR OF COMPLETION	1989
CLIENT	Technical and Secondary Education Construction Authority, Ministry of Education
ARCHITECT	José Sobral Blanco

Above: *main school entrance;* **Below:** *floor plan of resource centre.*

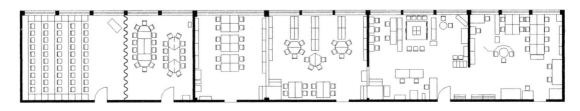

◀ public. It is an important facility for teachers and is used in adult education programmes.

The centre is an encouraging example of how educational facilities can be adapted at low cost to reflect and reinforce changes in society and of how they can make more effective use of the space at their disposal to the mutual advantage of the school and the wider community.

Left: *clearing the old classroom;* **Right:** *library and computer room;* **Below:** *a study room.*

Design and/or Layout

Architectural Heritage

Urban Renewal

 ## Rural Areas

 ## Environmental Education

Maintenance

Energy Conservation

Space Utilisation

Reuse of Existing Buildings

Information Technology

Lifelong Learning

Community

Business and Industry

Index
of architects

OECD Publications

AUSTRALIA
D.A. Information Services
648 Whitehorse Road, P.O.B. 163
Mitcham, Victoria 3132
Tel: (03) 9210 7777
Telefax: (03) 9210 7788

AUSTRIA
Gerold & Co.
Graben 31
Wien I
Tel: (0222) 533 50 14
Telefax: (0222) 512 47 31 29

BELGIUM
Jean De Lannoy
Avenue du Roi 202
B-1060 Bruxelles
Tel: (02) 538 51 69/538 08 41
Telfax: (02) 538 08 41

CANADA
Renouf Publishing Company Ltd.
1294 Algoma Road
Ottawa, ON K1B 3W8
Tel: (613) 741 4333
Telfax: (613) 741 5439

Stores:
61 Sparks Street
Ottawa, ON K1P 5R1
Tel: (613) 238 8985

12 Adelaide Street West
Toronto, ON M5H 1L6
Tel: (416) 363 3171
Telefax: (416) 363 5963

Les Editions La Liberté Inc.
3020 Chemin Sainte-Foy
Sainte-Foy, PQ G1X 3V6
Tel: (418) 658 3763
Telefax: (418) 658 3763

Federal Publications Inc.
165 University Avenue, Suite 701
Toronto, ON M5H 3B8
Tel: (416) 860 1611
Telefax: (416) 860 1608

Les Publications Fédérales
1185 Université
Montréal, QC H3B 3A7
Tel: (514) 954 1633
Telefax: (514) 954 1635

CHINA
China National Publications Import
Export Corporation (CNPIEC)
16 Gongti E. Road, Chaoyang District
P.O. Box 88 or 50
Beijing 100704 PR
Tel: (01) 506 6688
Telefax: (01) 506 3101

CHINESE TAIPEI
Good Faith Worldwide Int'l. Co. Ltd.
9th Floor, No. 118, Sec. 2
Chung Hsiao E. Road
Taipei
Tel: (02) 391 7396/391 7397
Telefax: (02) 394 9176

DENMARK
Munksgaard Book and Subscription
Service
35, Nørre Søgade, P.O. Box 2148
DK-1016 København K
Tel: (33) 12 85 70
Telefax: (33) 12 93 87

J.H. Schultz Information A/S
Herstedvang 12,
DK-2620 Albertslung
Tel: 43 63 23 00
Telefax: 43 63 19 69
Internet: s-info@inet.uni-c.dk

EGYPT
Middle East Observer
41 Sherif Street
Cairo
Tel: 392 6919
Telefax: 360 6804

FINLAND
Akateeminen Kirjakauppa
Keskuskatu 1, P.O. Box 128
00100 Helsinki

Subscription Services
P.O. Box 23
00371 Helsinki
Tel: (358 0) 121 4416
Telefax: (358 0) 121 4450

FRANCE
OECD
Mail Orders
2 rue André-Pascal
75775 Paris Cedex 16
Tel: (33-1) 45 24 82 00
Telefax: (33-1) 49 10 42 76
Telex: 640048 OCDE
Internet: Compte.PUBSINQ@oecd.org

Orders via Minitel, France only
3615 OCDE

OECD Bookshop
33, rue Octave-Feuillet
75016 Paris
Tel: (33-1) 45 24 81 81
(33-1) 45 24 81 67

Dawson
B.P. 40
91121 Palaiseau Cedex
Tel: 69 10 47 00
Telefax: 64 54 83 26

Documentation Française
29, quai Voltaire
75007 Paris
Tel: 40 15 70 00

Economica
49, rue Héricart
75015 Paris
Tel: 45 78 12 92
Telefax: 40 58 15 70

Gibert Jeune (Droit-Economie)
6, place Saint-Michel
75006 Paris
Tel: 43 25 91 19

Librairie du Commerce International
10, avenue d'Iéna
75016 Paris
Tel: 40 73 34 60

Librairie Dunod
Université Paris-Dauphine
Place du Maréchal de Lattre de Tassigny
75016 Paris
Tel: 44 05 40 13

Librairie Lavoisier
11, rue Lavoisier
75008 Paris
Tel: 42 65 39 95

Librairie des Sciences Politiques
30, rue Saint-Guillaume
75007 Paris
Tel: 45 48 36 02

P.U.F.
49, boulevard Saint-Michel
75005 Paris
Tel: 43 25 83 40

Librairie de l'Université
12a, rue Nazareth
13100 Aix-en-Provence
Tel: (16) 42 26 18 08

Documentation Française
165, rue Garibaldi
69003 Lyon
Tel: (16) 78 63 32 23

Librairie Decitre
29, place Bellecour
69002 Lyon
Tel: (16) 72 40 54 54

Librairie Sauramps
Le Triangle
34967 Montpellier Cedex 2
Tel: (16) 67 58 85 15
Telefax: (16) 67 58 27 36

A la Sorbonne Actual
23, rue de l'Hôtel-des-Postes
06000 Nice
Tel: (16) 93 13 77 75
Telefax: (16) 93 80 75 69

GERMANY
OECD Publications and Information
Centre
August-Bebel-Allee 6
D-53175 Bonn
Tel: (0228) 959 120
Telefax: (0228) 959 12 17

GREECE
Librairie Kauffmann
Mavrokordatou 9
106 78 Athens
Tel: (01) 32 55 321
Telefax: (01) 32 20 320

HONG KONG
Swindon Book Co. Ltd.
Astoria Bldg. 3F
34 Ashley Road, Tsimshatsui
Kowloon
Tel: 2376 2062
Telefax: 2376 0685

HUNGARY
Euro Info Service
Margitsziget, Európa Ház
1138 Budapest
Tel: (1) 111 62 16
Telefax: (1) 111 60 61

ICELAND
Mál Mog Menning
Laugavegi 18, Pósthólf 392
121 Reykjavik
Tel: (1) 552 4240
Telefax: (1) 562 3523

INDIA
Oxford Book and Stationery Co.
Scindia House
New Delhi 110001
Tel: (11) 331 5896/5308
Telefax: (11) 332 5993

17 Park Street
Calcutta 700016
Tel: 240832

INDONESIA
Pdii-Lipi
P.O. Box 4298
Jakarta 12042
Tel: (21) 573 34 67
Telefax: (21) 573 34 67

IRELAND
Government Supplies Agency
Publications Section
4/5 Harcourt Road
Dublin 2
Tel: 661 31 11
Telefax: 475 27 60

ISRAEL
Praedicta
5 Shatner Street
P.O. Box 34030
Jerusalem 91430
Tel: (2) 52 84 90/1/2
Telefax: (2) 52 84 93

R.O.Y. International
P.O. Box 13056
Tel Aviv 61130
Tel: (3) 546 1423
Telefax: (3) 546 1442

Palestinian Authority/Middle East
INDEX Information Services
P.O.B. 19502
Jerusalem
Tel: (2) 27 12 19
Telefax: (2) 27 16 34

ITALY
Libreria Commissionaria Sansoni
Via Duca di Calabria 1/1
50125 Firenze
Tel: (055) 64 54 15
Telefax: (055) 64 12 57

Via Bartolini 29
20155 Milano
Tel: (02) 36 50 83

Editrice e Libreria Herder
Piazza Montecitorio 120
00186 Roma
Tel: 679 46 28
Telefax: 678 47 51

Libreria Hoepli
Via Hoepli 5
20121 Milano
Tel: (02) 86 54 46
Telefax: (02) 805 28 86

Libreria Scientifica
Dott. Lucio de Biasio 'Aeiou'
Via Coronelli, 6
20146 Milano
Tel: (02) 48 95 45 52
Telefax: (02) 48 95 45 48

JAPAN
OECD Publications and
Information Centre
Landic Akasaka Building
2-3-4 Akasaka, Minato-ku
Tokyo 107
Tel: (81-3) 3586 2016
Telefax: (81-3) 3584 7929

KOREA
Kyobo Book Centre Co.Ltd.
P.O. Box 1658, Kwang Hwa Moon
Seoul
Tel: 730 78 91
Telefax: 735 00 30

MALAYSIA
University of Malaya Bookshop
University of Malaya
P.O. Box 1127, Jalan Pantai Baru
59700 Kuala Lumpur
Tel: 756 5000/756 5425
Telefax: 756 3246

MEXICO
OECD Publications and
Information Centre
Edificio INFOTEC
Av. San Fernando no.37
Col. Toriello Guerra
Tlalpan C.P. 14050
Mexico D.F.
Tel: (525) 606 00 11 ext.100
Telefax: (525) 606 13 07

Revistas y Periodicos Internacionales S.A.
de C.V.
Florencia 57 - 1004
Mexico D.F. 06600
Tel: 207 81 00
Telefax: 208 39 79

NETHERLANDS
SDU Uitgeverij Plantijnstraat
Externe Fondsen
Postbus 20014
2500 EA s'Gravenhage
Tel: (070) 37 89 880
Voor bestellingen:
Telefax: (070) 34 75 778

NEW ZEALAND
GP Legislation Services
P.O. Box 12418
Thorndon, Wellington
Tel: (04) 496 5655
Telefax: (04) 496 5698

NORWAY
NIC INFO A/S
Bertrand Narvesens vei 2
P.O. Box 6512 Etterstad
0606 Oslo 6
Tel: (022) 57 33 00
Telefax: (022) 68 19 01

PAKISTAN
Mirza Book Agency
65 Shahrah Quaid-E-Azam
Lahore 54000
Tel: (42) 735 36 01
Telefax: (42) 576 37 14

PHILLIPPINES
International Booksource Centre Inc.
Rm 179/920 Cityland 10 Condo Tower 2
HV de la Costa Ext cor Valero St.
Makati Metro Manila
Tel: (632) 817 9676
Telefax: (632) 817 1741

POLAND
Ars Polona
00-950 Warszawa
Krakowskie Przedmieácie 7
Tel: (22) 264760
Telefax: (22) 268673

PORTUGAL
Livraria Portugal
Rua do Carmo 70-74
Apart. 2681
1200 Lisboa
Tel: (01) 347 49 82/5
Telefax: (01) 347 02 64

SINGAPORE
Gower Asia Pacific Pte Ltd.
Golden Wheel Building
41, Kallang Pudding Road, No.04-03
Singapore 1334
Tel: 741 5166
Telefax: 742 9356

SPAIN
Mundi-Prensa Libros S.A.
Castelló 37, Apartado 1223
Madrid 28001
Tel: (91) 431 33 99
Telefax: (91) 575 39 98

Mundi-Prensa Barcelona
Consell de Cent No. 391
08009 Barcelona
Tel: (93) 488 34 92
Telefax: (93) 487 76 59

Llibreria de la Generalitat
Palau Moja
Rambla dels Estudis, 118
08002 Barcelona
(Subscripcions) Tel: (93) 318 80 12
(Publicacions) Tel: (93) 302 67 23
Telefax: (93) 412 18 54

SRI LANKA
Centre for Policy Research
c/o Colombo Agencies Ltd.
No. 300-304 Galle Road
Colombo 3
Tel: (1) 574240, 573551-2
Telefax: (1) 575394, 510711

SWEDEN
CE Fritzes AB
S-106 47 Stockholm
Tel: (08) 690 90 90
Telefax: (08) 20 50 21

Subscription Agency
Wennergren-Williams Info AB
P.O. Box 1305
171 25 Solna
Tel: (08) 705 97 50
Telefax: (08) 27 00 71

SWITZERLAND
Maditec S.A. (Books and Periodicals)
Chemin des Palettes 4
Case postale 266
1020 Renens VD 1
Tel: (021) 635 08 65
Telefax: (021) 635 07 80

Librairie Payot S.A.
4, place Pépinet
CP 3212
1002 Lausanne
Tel: (021) 320 25 11
Telefax: (021) 320 25 14

Librairie Unilivres
6, rue de Candolle
1205 Genève
Tel: (022) 320 26 23
Telefax: (022) 329 73 18

Subscription Agency
Dynapresse Marketing S.A.
38, avenue Vibert
1227 Carouge
Tel: (022) 308 07 89
Telefax: (022) 308 07 99

See also :
OECD Bonn Centre
August-Bebel-Allee 6
D-53175 Bonn (Germany)
Tel: (0228) 959 120
Telefax: (0228) 959 12 17

THAILAND
Suksit Siam Co. Ltd.
113, 115 Fuang Nakhon Rd.
Opp. Wat Rajbopith
Bangkok 10200
Tel: (662) 225 9531/2
Telefax: (662) 222 5188

TRINIDAD & TOBAGO
SSL Systematics Studies Limited
9 Watts Street
Curepe
Trinidad & Tobago, W. I.
Tel: (1809) 645 3475
Telefax: (1809) 662 5654

TUNISIA
Grande Librairie Spécialisée
Fendri Ali
Avenue Haffouz Imm El-Intilaka
Bloc B 1 Sfax 3000
Tel: (216-4) 296 855
Telefax: (216-4) 298 270

TURKEY
Kültür Yayinlari Is-Türk Ltd. Sti.
Atatürk Bulvari No. 191/Kat 13
Kavaklidere/Ankara
Tel: (312) 428 11 40 Ext.2458
Telefax: (312) 417 24 90

Dolmabahce Cad. No.29
Besiktas/Istanbul
Tel: (212) 260 7188

UNITED KINGDOM
HMSO
General enquiries: Tel: (171) 873 8242
Postal orders only:
P.O.Box 276
London SW8 5DT
Telefax: (171) 873 8416
Personal callers:
HMSO Bookshop
49 High Holborn
London WC1V 6HB

Branches at: Belfast, Birmingham,
Bristol, Edinburgh, Manchester

UNITED STATES
OECD Publications and Information
Centre
2001 L Street N.W., Suite 650
Washington D.C. 20036-4922
Tel: (202) 785 6323
Telefax: (202) 785 0350
Internet: washcont@oecd.org

Subscriptions to OECD periodicals may
also be placed through main
subscription agencies.

Orders and enquiries from countries
where Distributors have not yet been
appointed should be sent to OECD
Publications Service, 2 rue André-
Pascal, 75775 Paris Cedex 16, France.

5-1996

OECD PUBLICATIONS, 2 rue André-Pascal, 75775 PARIS CEDEX 16
PRINTED IN FRANCE
(95 96 05 1) ISBN 92-64-15291-1 – No. 49017 1996